NARRATIVE

OF THE

MUTINY OF THE BOUNTY,

ON

A Voyage to the South Seas.

BY

LIEUT. W. BLIGH, COMMANDER.

TO WHICH ARE ADDED

SOME ADDITIONAL PARTICULARS, AND A RELATION OF THE SUBSEQUENT FATE OF THE
MUTINEERS, AND OF THE SETTLEMENT IN PITCAIRN'S ISLAND.

THE
MUTINY OF THE BOUNTY.

CHAPTER I.

THE king having been graciously pleased to comply with a request from the merchants and planters interested in his majesty's West India possessions, that the bread-fruit tree might be introduced into those islands, a vessel, proper for the undertaking, was bought, and taken into dock at Deptford, to be provided with the necessary fixtures and preparations for executing the object of the voyage. These were completed according to a plan of my much honoured friend, Sir Joseph Banks, which, in the event, proved the most advantageous that could have been adopted for the intended purpose.

The ship was named the Bounty: I was appointed to command her on the 16th of August, 1787. Her burthen was nearly two hundred and fifteen tons; her extreme length on deck, ninety feet ten inches; extreme breadth, twenty-four feet three inches; and height in the hold under the beams, at the main hatchway, ten feet three inches. In the cockpit were the cabins of the surgeon, gunner, botanist, and clerk, with a steward-room and store-rooms. The between decks was divided in the following manner:—the great cabin was appropriated for the preservation of the plants, and extended as far forward as the after hatchway. It had two large sky-lights, and on each side three scuttles for air, and was fitted with a false floor cut full of holes to contain the garden-pots, in which the plants were to be brought home. The deck was covered with lead, and at the foremost corners of the cabin were fixed pipes to carry off the water that drained from the plants, into tubs placed below to save it for future use. I had a small cabin on one side to sleep in, adjoining to the great cabin, and a place near the middle of the ship to eat in. The bulk-head of this apartment was at the after-part of the main hatchway, and on each side of it were the births of the mates and midshipmen; between these births the arm-chest was placed. The cabin of the master, in which was always kept the key of the arms, was opposite to mine. This particular description of the interior parts of the ship is rendered necessary by the event of the expedition.

The ship was masted according to the proportion of the navy; but, on my application, the masts were shortened, as I thought them too much for her, considering the nature of the voyage.

On the 3rd of September, the ship came out of dock; but the carpenters and joiners remained on board much longer, as they had a great deal of work to finish.

The next material alteration made in the fitting out, was, lessening the quantity of iron and other ballast.—I gave directions that only nineteen tons of iron should be taken on board, instead of the customary proportion, which was forty-five tons. The stores and provisions I judged would be fully sufficient to answer the purpose of the remainder; for I am of opinion, that many of the misfortunes which attend ships in heavy storms of wind, are occasioned by too much dead weight in their bottoms.

The establishment of men and officers for the ship were as follows:—1 Lieutenant to command; 1 Master; 1 Boatswain; 1 Gunner; 1 Carpenter; 1 Surgeon; 2 Master's Mates; 2 Midshipmen; 2 Quarter Masters; 1 Quarter Masters' Mate; 1 Boatswain's Mate; 1 Gunner's Mate; 1 Carpenter's Mate; 1 Carpenter's Crew; 1 Sailmaker; 1 Armourer; 1 Corporal; 1 Clerk and Steward; 23 able seamen—Total 44.

Two skilful and careful men were appointed, at Sir Joseph Banks's recommendation, to have the management of the plants intended to be brought home: the one, David Nelson, who had been on similar employment in Captain Cook's last voyage; the other, William Brown, as an assistant to him.—With these two, our whole number amounted to forty-six.

It was proposed, that our route to the Society Islands should be round Cape Horn; and the greatest despatch became necessary, as the season was already far advanced: but the shipwrights not being able to complete their work by the time the ship was ready in other respects, our sailing was unavoidably retarded. However, by the 4th of October the pilot came on board to take us down the river; on the 9th we fell down to Long Reach, where we received our gunner's stores, and guns, four 4-pounders and ten swivels.

The ship was stored and victualled for eighteen months. In addition to the customary allowance of provisions, we were supplied with sour krout, portable soup, essence of malt, dried malt, and a proportion of barley and wheat in lieu of oatmeal. I was likewise furnished with a quantity of iron-work and trinkets, to serve in our intercourse with the natives in the South Seas; and from the Board of Longitude I received a time-keeper, made by Mr. Kendal.

On the 15th I received orders to proceed to

B 2

Spithead; but the winds and weather were so unfavourable that we did not arrive there till the 4th of November. On the 24th I received from Lord Hood, who commanded at Spithead, my final orders. The wind, which for several days before had been favourable, was now turned directly against us. On the 28th the ship's company received two months' pay in advance, and on the following morning we worked out to St. Helen's, where we were obliged to anchor.

We made different unsuccessful attempts to get down channel, but contrary winds and bad weather constantly forced us back to St. Helen's, or Spithead, until Sunday the 23rd of December, when we sailed with a fair wind.

The object of all the former voyages to the South Seas, undertaken by the command of his present majesty, has been the advancement of science, and the increase of knowledge. This voyage may be reckoned the first, the intention of which has been to derive benefit from those distant discoveries. For the more fully comprehending the nature and plan of the expedition, and that the reader may be possessed of every information necessary for entering on the following sheets, I shall here lay before him a copy of the instructions I received from the Admiralty, and likewise a short description of the bread-fruit.

By the Commissioners for executing the office of Lord High Admiral of Great Britain and Ireland, &c.

Whereas the king, upon a representation from the merchants and planters interested in his majesty's West India possessions, that the introduction of the bread-fruit tree into the islands of those seas, to constitute an article of food, would be of very essential benefit to the inhabitants, hath, in order to promote the interests of so respectable a body of his subjects (especially in an instance which promises general advantage) thought fit that measures should be taken for the procuring some of those trees, and conveying them to the said West India islands: and whereas the vessel under your command hath, in consequence thereof, been stored and victualled for that service, and fitted with proper conveniences and necessaries for the preservation of as many of the said trees as, from her size, can be taken on board her: and you have been directed to receive on board her the two gardeners named in the margin*, who, from their knowledge of trees and plants, have been hired for the purpose of selecting such as shall appear to be of a proper species and size:

You are, therefore, in pursuance of his majesty's pleasure, signified to us by Lord Sydney, one of his principal secretaries of state, hereby required and directed to put to sea in the vessel you command, the first favourable opportunity of wind and weather, and proceed with her, as expeditiously as possible, round Cape Horn, to the Society Islands, situate in the southern ocean, in the latitude of about eighteen degrees south, and longitude of about two hundred and ten degrees east from Greenwich, where, according to the accounts given by the late Capt. Cook, and persons who accompanied him during his voyages, the bread-fruit tree is to be found in the most luxuriant state.

Having arrived at the above-mentioned islands, and taken on board as many trees and plants as may be thought necessary (the better to enable you to do which, you have already been furnished with such articles of merchandise and trinkets as it is supposed will be wanted to satisfy the natives) you are to proceed from thence through Endeavour Straights (which separate New Holland from New Guinea) to Prince's Island, in the Straights of Sunda, or, if it should happen to be more convenient, to pass on the

* David Nelson, William Brown.

eastern side of Java to some port on the north side of that island, where any bread-fruit trees which may have been injured, or have died, may be replaced by mangosteens, duriens, jacks, nancas, lansie, and other fine fruit trees of that quarter, as well as the rice plant which grows upon dry land; all of which species (or such of them as shall be judged most eligible) you are to purchase on the best terms you can from the inhabitants of that island, with the ducats with which you have also been furnished for that purpose; taking care, however, if the rice plants above-mentioned cannot be procured at Java, to touch at Prince's Island for them, where they are regularly cultivated.

From Prince's Island, or the Island of Java, you are to proceed round the Cape of Good Hope to the West Indies (calling on your way thither at any places which may be thought necessary) and deposit one half of such of the above-mentioned trees and plants as may be then alive at his majesty's botanical garden at St. Vincent, for the benefit of the Windward Islands, and then go on to Jamaica: and, having delivered the remainder to Mr. East, or such person or persons as may be authorised by the governor and council of that island to receive them; refreshed your people, and received on board such provisions and stores as may be necessary for the voyage, make the best of your way back to England: repairing to Spithead, and sending to our secretary an account of your arrival and proceedings.

And whereas you will receive herewith a copy of the instructions which have been given to the above-mentioned gardeners for their guidance, as well in procuring the said trees and plants, and the management of them after they shall be put on board, as for bringing to England a small sample of each species, and such others as may be prepared by the superintendant of the botanical garden at St. Vincent's, and by the said Mr. East, or others, for his majesty's garden at Kew; you are hereby required and directed to afford, and to give directions to your officers and company to afford, the said gardeners every possible aid and assistance, not only in the collecting of the said trees and plants at the places before-mentioned, but for their preservation during their conveyance to the places of their destination.

Given under our hands the 20th November, 1787.—Howe, Chas. Brett, Rd. Hopkins, J. Leveson Gower.

To Lieut. W. Bligh, commanding H.M.'s armed vessel the Bounty, at Spithead.

By command of their Lordships,   P. Stevens.

In the foregoing orders it is to be observed, that I was particularly directed to proceed round Cape Horn; but, as the season was so far advanced, and we were so long detained by contrary winds, I made application to the Admiralty for discretional orders on that point; to which I received the following answer:—

By the Commissioners for executing the office of Lord High Admiral of Great Britain and Ireland, &c. &c.

The season of the year being now so far advanced as to render it probable, that your arrival, with the vessel you command, on the southern coast of America, will be too late for your passing round Cape Horn without much difficulty and hazard; you are, in that case, at liberty (notwithstanding former orders) to proceed in her to Otaheite, round the Cape of Good Hope.

Given under our hands the 18th December, 1787.—Howe, Chas. Brett, Bayham.

To Lieut. W. Bligh, commanding H.M.'s armed vessel Bounty, Spithead.

By command of their Lordships,   P. Stevens.

The bread-fruit is so well known and described, that to attempt a new account of it would be unnecessary and useless. However, as it may contribute to the convenience of the reader, I have given the following extracts respecting it.

Extract from the account of Dampier's Voyage round the World, performed in 1688.

"The bread-fruit (as we call it,) grows on a large tree, as big and high as our largest apple-trees. It hath a spreading head, full of branches and dark leaves. The fruit grows on the boughs like apples; it is as big as a penny-loaf when wheat is at five shillings the bushel; it is of a round shape, and hath a thick tough rind. When the fruit is ripe, it is yellow and soft, and the taste is sweet and pleasant. The natives of Guam use it for bread. They gather it, when full-grown, while it is green and hard; then they bake it in an oven, which scorcheth the rind and makes it black; but they scrape off the outside black crust, and there remains a tender thin crust; and the inside is soft, tender, and white like the crumb of a penny-loaf. There is *neither seed nor stone* in the inside, but all is of a pure substance, like bread. It must be eaten new; for, if it is kept above twenty-four hours, it grows harsh and choaky; but it is very pleasant before it is too stale. This fruit lasts in season *eight months* in the year, during which the natives eat *no other sort of food of bread kind.* I did never see of this fruit any where but here. The natives told us, that there is plenty of this fruit growing on the rest of the Ladrone islands: and I *did never hear of it any where else.*"

Extract from the account of Lord Anson's Voyage, published by Mr. Walter.

"There was, at Tinian, a kind of fruit, peculiar to these (Ladrone) islands, called by the Indians *rhymay*, but by us the *bread-fruit*; for it was constantly eaten by us, during our stay upon the island*, instead of bread; and so *universally preferred*, that no ship's bread was expended in that whole interval. It grew upon a tree which is somewhat lofty, and which towards the top divides into large and spreading branches. The leaves of this tree are of a remarkable deep green, are notched about the edges, and are generally from a foot to eighteen inches in length. The fruit itself is found indifferently on all parts of the branches; it is, in shape, rather elliptical than round; it is covered with a tough rind, and is usually seven or eight inches long; each of them grows singly, and not in clusters. This fruit is fittest to be used when it is full-grown, but still green; in which state, after it is properly prepared by being roasted in the embers, its taste has some distant resemblance to that of an artichoke's bottom, and its texture is not very different, for it is soft and spungy."

Extracts from the account of the first Voyage of Captain Cook. Hawkesworth, Vol. II.

IN THE SOCIETY ISLANDS.

"The bread-fruit grows on a tree that is about the size of a middling oak; its leaves are frequently a foot and a half long, of an oblong shape, deeply sinuated like those of the fig-tree, which they resemble in consistence and colour, and in the exuding of a white milky juice upon being broken. The fruit is about the size and shape of a child's head, and the surface is reticulated not much un-

* About two months; viz. from the latter end of August to the latter end of October, 1742.

like a truffle: it is covered with a thin skin, and has a core about as big as the handle of a small knife. The eatable part lies between the skin and the core; it is as white as snow, and somewhat of the consistence of new bread: it must be roasted before it is eaten, being first divided into three or four parts. Its taste is insipid, with a slight sweetness somewhat resembling that of the crumb of wheaten bread mixed with a Jerusalem artichoke."

"Of the many vegetables that have been mentioned already as serving them for food, the principal is the bread-fruit, to procure which costs them no trouble or labour but climbing a tree. The tree which produces it does not indeed shoot up spontaneously; but, if a man plants ten of them in his life-time, which he may do in about an hour, he will as completely fulfil his duty to his own and future generations as the native of our less temperate climate can do by ploughing in the cold winter, and reaping in the summer's heat, as often as these seasons return; even if, after he has procured bread for his present household, he should convert a surplus into money, and lay it up for his children."

"It is true, indeed, that the bread-fruit is not always in season; but cocoa-nuts, bananas, plantains, and a great variety of other fruits, supply the deficiency."

Extract from the account of Captain Cook's last Voyage.

IN THE SOCIETY ISLANDS.

"I (Captain Cook) have inquired very carefully into their manner of cultivating the bread-fruit tree at Otaheite; but was always answered, that they never planted it. This, indeed, must be evident to every one who will examine the places where the young trees come up. It will be always observed, that they spring from the roots of the old ones, which run along near the surface of the ground. So that the bread-fruit trees may be reckoned those that would naturally cover the plains, even supposing that the island was not inhabited; in the same manner that the white-barked trees, found at Van Diemen's Land, constitute the forests there. And from this we may observe, that the inhabitant of Otaheite, instead of being obliged to plant his bread, will *rather* be under the necessity of preventing its progress; which, I suppose, is sometimes done, to give room for trees of another sort, to afford him some variety in his food."

IN THE SANDWICH ISLANDS.

"The bread-fruit trees are planted, and flourish with great luxuriance, on rising grounds."—"Where the hills rise almost perpendicularly in a great variety of peaked forms, their steep sides and the deep chasms between them are covered with trees, amongst which those of the bread-fruit were observed particularly to abound."

"The climate of the Sandwich Islands differs very little from that of the West India Islands, which lie *in the same latitude*. Upon the whole, perhaps, it may be rather more temperate."

"The bread-fruit trees thrive in these islands, not in such abundance, but produce double the quantity of fruit they do on the rich plains of Otaheite. The trees are nearly of the same height, but the branches begin to strike out from the trunk much lower, and with greater luxuriance."

CHAPTER II.

DEPARTURE FROM ENGLAND—ARRIVAL AT TENERIFFE—SAIL FROM THENCE—ARRIVAL OFF CAPE HORN—SEVERITY OF THE WEATHER—OBLIGED TO BEAR AWAY FOR THE CAPE OF GOOD HOPE.

On Sunday morning, the 23d of December 1787, we sailed from Spithead, and, passing through the Needles, directed our course down channel, with a fresh gale of wind at east. In the afternoon one of the seamen, in furling the main-top-gallant sail, fell off the yard, and was so fortunate as to save himself by catching hold of the main-top-mast-stay in his fall. At night the wind increased to a strong gale, with a heavy sea. It moderated, however, on the 25th, and allowed us to keep our Christmas with cheerfulness; but the following day it blew a severe storm of wind from the eastward, which continued till the 29th, in the course of which we suffered greatly. One sea broke away the spare yards and spars out of the starboard main chains. Another heavy sea broke into the ship, and stove all the boats. Several casks of beer that had been lashed upon deck were broke loose and washed overboard, and it was not without great difficulty and risk that we were able to secure the boats from being washed away entirely. On the 29th we were in latitude 39° 35' N. and longitude 14° 26' W. when the gale abated, and the weather became fair. Besides other mischief done to us by the storm, a large quantity of our bread was damaged and rendered useless, for the sea had stove in our stern, and filled the cabin with water. From this time to our arrival at Teneriffe we had moderate weather, and winds mostly from the northward.

January 4th. This forenoon we spoke a French ship bound to the Mauritius. The next day, at nine in the forenoon, we saw the island of Teneriffe, bearing W.S.W. ¼ W. about twelve leagues distant. It was covered with a thick haze, except the north-westernmost part, which is a remarkable headland, resembling a horse's head, the ears very distinct. To the eastward of this head lie two round rocks, the northern boundary of Teneriffe. A Spanish packet, bound to Corunna, an American brig, and several other vessels, were lying here. As soon as the ship was anchored, I sent an officer (Mr. Christian) to wait on the governor, and to acquaint him I had put in to obtain refreshments, and to repair the damages we had sustained in bad weather. To this I had a very polite answer from the governor*, that I should be supplied with whatever the island afforded. I had also directed the officer to acquaint him that I would salute, provided an equal number of guns were to be returned; but, as I received an extraordinary answer to this part of my message, purporting that his excellency did not return the same number but to persons equal in rank to himself, this ceremony was omitted.

During this interval I was visited by the portmaster (Captain Adams), and shortly afterwards several officers came on board from his excellency, to compliment me on my arrival. As soon as the ship was moored, I went on shore, and paid my respects to him.

On Monday morning I began to forward the ship's business with the utmost dispatch, and gave the necessary directions to Messrs. Collogan and Sons, the contractors, for the supplies I wanted. I also got leave of the governor for Mr. Nelson to range the hills and examine the country in search of plants and natural curiosities.

As there was a great surf on the shore, I bargained for every thing I wanted to be brought off by the shore boats, and agreed to give five shillings per ton for water. Very good wine was bought at ten pounds per pipe, the contract price; but the superior quality was fifteen pounds; and some of this was not much inferior to the best London Madeira. I found this was an unfavourable season for other refreshments: Indian corn, potatoes, pumpkins, and onions, were all very scarce, and double the price of what they are in summer. Beef also was difficult to be procured, and exceedingly poor; the price nearly sixpence farthing per pound. The corn was three current dollars per fanega, which is full five shillings per bushel; and biscuit at twenty-five shillings for the hundred pounds. Poultry was so scarce that a good fowl cost three shillings. This is, therefore, not a place for ships to expect refreshments at a reasonable price at this time of the year, wine excepted; but from March to November supplies are plentiful, particularly fruit; of which at this time we could procure none, except a few dried figs and some bad oranges.

The landing on the beach is generally impracticable with our own boats, at least without great risk; but there is a very fine pier, on which people may land without difficulty if there is not much swell in the road. To this pier the water is conveyed by pipes for the use of shipping, and for which all merchant-ships pay.

There is a degree of wretchedness and want among the lower class of people, which is not any where so common as among the Spanish and Portuguese settlements. To alleviate these evils, the present governor of Teneriffe has instituted a most charitable society, which he takes the trouble to superintend; and by considerable contributions, a large airy dwelling, that contains one hundred and twenty poor girls, and as many men and boys, has been built, and endowed with a sufficiency of land round it, not only for all present purposes, but for enlarging the building for more objects of charity as their funds increase. I had the honour to be shown by his excellency this asylum, (Hospicio they call it,) where there appeared in every countenance the utmost cheerfulness and content. The decency and neatness of the dress of the young females, with the order in which they were arranged at their spinning-wheels and looms, in an extensive airy apartment, was admirable. A governess inspected and regulated all their works, which were the manufacturing of ribbons of all colours, coarse linens, and tapes; all which were managed and brought to perfection by themselves, from the silk and flax in their first state; even the dyeing of the colours is performed by them. These girls are received for five years, at the end of which they are at liberty to marry, and have for their portions their wheel and loom, with a sum of money proportioned to the state of the fund, which is assisted by the produce of their labour, and at this time was estimated at two thousand dollars per annum.

---

* Marquis de Branchefort.

The men and boys are not less attended to: they are employed in coarser work, blanketing and all kinds of common woollens: if they become infirm, they spend the remainder of their days here comfortably, and under a watchful inspector, who attends them in the same manner as the governess does the girls. They are all visited every day by the governor, and a clergyman attends them every evening. By this humane institution a number of people are rendered useful and industrious, in a country where the poor, from the indulgence of the climate, are too apt to prefer a life of inactivity, though attended with wretchedness, to obtaining the comforts of life by industry and labour.

The number of inhabitants in the island, I was informed, were estimated at between eighty and one hundred thousand. Their annual export of wine is twenty thousand pipes, and of brandy half that quantity. Vessels are frequently here from St. Eustatia, and from thence a great quantity of Teneriffe wine is carried to the different parts of the West Indies, under the name of Madeira.

Teneriffe is considered of more value than all the other Canaries: the inhabitants, however, in scarce seasons receive supplies from the Grand Canary; but their vineyards here are said to be greatly superior. Their produce of corn, though exceedingly good, is not sufficient for their consumption; and, owing to this, the Americans have an advantageous trade here for their flour and grain, and take wine in return.

The town of Santa Cruz is about half a mile in extent each way, built in a regular manner, and the houses in general large and airy, but the streets are very ill paved. I am told that they are subject to few diseases; but if any epidemic distemper breaks out, it is attended with the most fatal consequences, particularly the small-pox, the bad effects of which they now endeavour to counteract by inoculation. For this reason they are very circumspect in admitting ships to have communication with the shore without bills of health.

A sloop from London, called the Chance, William Meredith, master, bound to Barbadoes, out nineteen days from the Downs, came into the road the day before we sailed. She had suffered much by the bad weather; but, having brought no bill of health, the governor would not allow any person to come on shore, unless I could vouch for them that no epidemic disease raged in England at the time they sailed, which I was able to do, it being nearly at the same time that I left the land; and by that means they had the governor's permission to receive the supplies they wanted, without being obliged to perform quarantine.

Having finished our business at Teneriffe, on Thursday the 10th, we sailed with the wind at S.E., our ship's company all in good health and spirits.

I now divided the people into three watches, and gave the charge of the third watch to Mr. Fletcher Christian, one of the mates.—I have always considered this as a desirable regulation, when circumstances will admit of it, on many accounts; and am persuaded that unbroken rest not only contributes much towards the health of a ship's company, but enables them more readily to exert themselves in cases of sudden emergency.

As it was my wish to proceed to Otaheite without stopping, I ordered every body to be at two-thirds allowance of bread; I also directed the water for drinking to be filtered through drip-stones that I had bought at Teneriffe for that purpose.

We ran all night towards the S.S.W., having the wind at S.E. The next morning we could see nothing of the land. I now made the ship's company acquainted with the intent of the voyage; and, having been permitted to hold out this encouragement to them, I gave assurances of the certainty of promotion to every one whose endeavours should merit it.

The winds, for some days after leaving Teneriffe, were mostly from the southward. Fishing-lines and tackle were distributed amongst the people, and some dolphins were caught.

On the 17th the wind came round to the N.E., and continued steady in that quarter till the 25th, on which day, at noon, we were in 5° 54' N. As the cloudiness of the sky gave us reason to expect much rain, we prepared the awnings with hoses for the convenience of saving water, in which we were not disappointed. From this time to our meeting with the S.E. trade wind we had much wet weather, the air close and sultry, with calms, and light variable winds, generally from the southward.

On the 29th there was so heavy a fall of rain that we caught seven hundred gallons of water.

On the 31st, latitude at noon, 2° 5' N., found a current setting to the N.E., at the rate of fourteen miles in the twenty-four hours. The thermometer was at 82° in the shade, and 81½° at the surface of the sea, so that the air and the water were within half a degree of the same temperature. At eight o'clock in the evening we observed a violent rippling in the sea, about half a mile to the N.W. of us, which had very much the appearance of breakers. This I imagine to have been occasioned by a large school (or multitude) of fish, as it was exactly in the track the ship had passed, so that if any real shoal had been there, we must have seen it at the close of the evening, when a careful look-out was always kept. However, if it had appeared ahead of us, instead of astern, I should certainly have tacked to avoid it. To such appearances I attribute the accounts of many shoals within the tropics, which cannot be found any where but in maps. Our latitude at this time was 2° 8' N., and longitude 19° 43' W. The next day we had more of these appearances, from the number of schools of fish by which the ship was surrounded.

Saturday the 2nd. This morning we saw a sail to the N.N.W., but at too great a distance to distinguish what she was.

Monday the 4th. Had very heavy rain; during which we nearly filled all our empty water casks. So much wet weather, with the closeness of the air, covered every thing with mildew. The ship was aired below with fires, and frequently sprinkled with vinegar; and every little interval of dry weather was taken advantage of to open all the hatchways, and clean the ship, and to have all the people's wet things washed and dried.

With this weather, and light unsteady winds, we advanced but 2½ degrees in twelve days; at the end of which time we were relieved by the S.E. trade wind, which we fell in with on the 6th at noon, in latitude 1° 21' N., and longitude 20° 42' W.

The next afternoon we crossed the equinoctial line, in longitude 21° 50' W. The weather became fine, and the S.E. trade wind was fresh and steady, with which we kept a point free from the wind, and got to the southward at a good rate.

The weather continuing dry, we put some of our bread in casks, properly prepared for its reception, to preserve it from vermin: this experiment, we afterwards found, answered exceedingly well.

On the 16th, at daylight, we saw a sail to the southward. The next day we came up with her, and found her to be the British Queen, Simon Paul, master, from London, bound to the Cape of Good Hope on the whale-fishery. She sailed from Falmouth the 5th of December, eighteen days before I left Spithead. By this ship I wrote to England. At sunset she was almost out of sight astern.

Monday the 18th. At noon we were in latitude 26° 44' S., and longitude 31° 23' W. In our advances towards the south, the wind had gradually veered round to the east, and was at this time at E.N.E. The weather, after crossing the Line, had been fine and clear, but the air so sultry as to occasion great faintness, the quicksilver in the thermometer, in the day-time, standing at between 81 and 83 degrees, and one time at 85 degrees. In our passage through the northern tropic, the air was temperate, the sun having then high south declination and the weather being generally fine till we lost the N.E. trade wind; but such a thick haze surrounded the horizon, that no object could be seen, except at a very small distance. The haze commonly cleared away at sunset, and gathered again at sunrise. Between the N.E. and S.E. trade winds, the calms and rains, if of long continuance, are very liable to produce sickness, unless great attention is paid to keeping the ship clean and wholesome, by giving all the air possible, drying between decks with fires, and drying and airing the people's clothes and bedding. Besides these precautions, we frequently wetted with vinegar; and every evening the pumps were used as ventilators. With these endeavours to secure health, we passed the low latitudes without a single complaint.

The currents we met with were by no means regular, nor have I ever found them so in the middle of the ocean. However, from the channel to the southward, as far as Madeira, there is generally a current setting to the S.S.E.

On the evening of the 21st, a ship was seen in the N.E., but at too great a distance to distinguish of what country. The next day the wind came round to the N. and N.W., so that we could no longer consider ourselves in the trade wind. Our latitude at noon was 25° 55' S., longitude 36° 29' W. Variation of the compass three degrees east.

Sat. 23rd, towards night the wind died away, and we had some heavy showers of rain, of which we profited, by saving a ton of good water. The next day we caught a shark and five dolphins.

Tuesday, 26th, we bent new sails, and made other necessary preparations for encountering the weather that was to be expected in a high latitude. Our latitude at noon was 29° 38' S., longitude 41° 44' W. Variation 7° 13' E. In the afternoon, the wind being westerly, and blowing strong in

squalls, some butterflies, and other insects, like what we call horse-flies, were blown on board of us. No birds were seen except shearwaters. Our distance from the coast of Brazil at this time was above 100 leagues.

Sunday, March 2nd, in the forenoon, after seeing that every person was clean, divine service was performed, according to my usual custom on this day. I gave to Mr. Fletcher Christian, whom I had before directed to take charge of the third watch, a written order to act as lieutenant.

Saturday, 8th. We were at noon in latitude 36° 50' S., and longitude 52° 52' W. The last four days, we several times tried for soundings, without finding bottom, though considerably to the westward of Captain Wallis's track, who had soundings at fifty-four fathoms depth, in latitude 35° 49' S., and longitude 49° 54' W. This day we tried with two hundred and forty fathoms of line, but did not find bottom; at the same time, observing a rippling in the water, we tried the current by mooring a keg with one hundred fathoms of line, by which it appeared to run to the N.N.W., at the rate of a mile and a half per hour. By the noon observation, however, we were eighteen miles to the southward of our reckoning. In the afternoon we saw a turtle floating, and, not having much wind, hoisted a boat out, and sent after it; but it was found to be in a putrid state, with a number of crabs feeding upon it.

The change of temperature began now to be sensibly felt, there being a variation in the thermometer, since yesterday, of eight degrees. That the people might not suffer by their own negligence, I gave orders for their light tropical clothing to be put by, and made them dress in a manner more suited to a cold climate. I had provided for this before I left England, by giving directions for such clothes to be purchased as were necessary.

Monday, 10th. In the forenoon we struck soundings at eighty-three fathoms depth; our latitude 40° 8' S., and longitude 55° 40' W. This I conclude to have been near the edge of the bank; for, the wind being at S.S.W., we stood towards the S.E.; and, after running fourteen miles in that direction, we could find no bottom with one hundred and sixty fathoms of line. In the night we stood towards the W.S.W., with a southerly wind, and got again into soundings. The next day we saw a great number of whales of an immense size, that had two spout-holes on the back of the head.—Upon a complaint made to me by the master, I found it necessary to punish Matthew Quintal, one of the seamen, with two dozen lashes, for insolence and mutinous behaviour. Before this, I had not had occasion to punish any person on board.

On the 12th, we caught a porpoise, by striking it with the grains. Every one ate heartily of it; and it was so well liked, that no part was wasted.

On the 14th, in the afternoon, we saw a land-bird like a lark, and passed part of a dead whale that had been left by some whalers after they had taken the blubber off. Saw, likewise, two strange sail.

On the 19th, at noon, by my account, we were within twenty leagues of Port Desire; but the wind blowing fresh from the N.W. with thick foggy weather, I did not attempt to make the land. We passed a good deal of rock-weed, and saw many whales, and albatrosses and other sea-birds.

On the 20th, in the afternoon, the wind, which had for some time past been northerly, suddenly shifted to the W.S.W. and blew hard. We steered to the S.S.E.; and on the 23rd, at two o'clock in the morning, we discovered the coast of Terra del Fuego bearing S.E. At nine in the forenoon we were off Cape St. Diego, the eastern part of Terra del Fuego. The wind being unfavourable, I thought it more advisable to go round to the eastward of Staten Land, than to attempt passing through Straits le Maire. The two opposite coasts of the Straits exhibited very different appearances. The land of Terra del Fuego hereabouts, though the interior parts are mountainous, yet near the coast is of a moderate height, and, at the distance we were from it, had not an unpromising appearance. The coast of Staten Land, near the Straits, is mountainous and craggy, and remarkable for its high peaked hills. Straits le Maire is a fair opening, which cannot well be mistaken; but if any doubt could remain, the different appearances of the opposite shores would sufficiently make the Straits known.

I did not sail within less than six leagues of the coast, that we might have the wind more regular, and avoid being exposed to the heavy squalls that came off from the land.

The sight of New Year's Harbour almost tempted me to put in; but the lateness of the season, and the people being in good health, determined me to lay aside all thoughts of refreshment, until we should reach Otaheite. At two o'clock in the afternoon, the easternmost of New Year's Isles, where Captain Cook observed the latitude to be 55° 40′ S., bore from us south four leagues. We saw the entrance isles of New Year's harbour; at the back of which the land is very craggy and mountainous. This must be a very convenient port to touch at, as the access to it is safe and easy.

About two leagues to the westward of Cape St. John, I observed the separation of the mountains that Captain Cook has taken notice of, which has the appearance of Staten Land being there divided into two islands.

Monday, 24th. We had stood to the southward all night, with the wind at W.S.W. and S.W. At eight in the morning, Cape St. John bore N.W., ten leagues distant. Soon after we lost sight of the land.

From the time we lost sight of the land, to the end of the month, we were struggling with bad weather and contrary winds: but on the morning of the 31st the wind came to the N.N.E., and made us entertain great hopes that we should be able to accomplish our passage round the Cape without much difficulty. At noon we were in latitude 60° 1′ S., and in 71° 45′ W. longitude, which is 8° 26′ W. of the meridian of Cape St. John. This flattering appearance was not of long continuance: in the night the wind became variable, and next day settled again in the W. and N.W., with very bad weather.

On April 2nd, in the morning, the wind, which had blown fresh all night from the N.W., came round to the S.W., and increased to a heavy gale. At six in the morning the storm exceeded what I had ever met with before; and the sea, from the frequent shifting of the wind, running in contrary directions, broke exceeding high. Our ship, however, lay to very well, under a main and fore stay-sail. The gale continued, with severe squalls of hail and sleet, the remainder of this, and all the next day.—On the 4th, the wind was less violent, but far from moderate. With so much bad weather, I found it necessary to keep a constant fire, night and day; and one of the watch always attended to dry the people's wet clothes: and this, I have no doubt, contributed as much to their health as to their comfort.

Our companions in this inhospitable region, were albatrosses, and two beautiful kinds of birds, the small blue petterel, and pintada. A great many of these were frequently about the wake of the ship, which induced the people to float a line with hooks baited, to endeavour to catch them; and their attempts were successful. The method they used, was to fasten the bait a foot or two before the hook, and, by giving the line a sudden jerk when the bird was at the bait, it was hooked in the feet or body.

On the 6th the weather was moderate, and continued so till the 9th, with the wind veering between the N.W. and S.W.; of which we were able to take advantage.

On the 10th we saw some fish, which appeared spotted, and about the size of bonetos: these were the only fish we had seen in this high latitude.

The stormy weather continued with a great sea. The ship now began to complain, and required to be pumped every hour; which was no more than we had reason to expect from such a continuance of gales and high seas. The decks also became so leaky, that I was obliged to allot the great cabin, of which I made little use, except in fine weather, to those people who had wet births, to hang their hammocks in; and by this means the between-decks was less crowded.

Every morning all the hammocks were taken down from where they hung, and when the weather was too bad to keep them upon deck, they were put in the cabin; so that the between-decks were cleaned daily, and aired with fires, if the hatchways could not be opened. With all this bad weather, we had the additional mortification to find, at the end of every day, that we were losing ground; for notwithstanding our utmost exertions, and keeping on the most advantageous tacks, (which, if the weather had been at all moderate, would have sufficiently answered our purpose) yet the greater part of the time, we were doing little better than drifting before the wind.

Birds, as usual, were about the ship, and some of them caught; and, for the first time since we left Staten Land, we saw some whales. This morning, owing to the violent motion of the ship, the cook fell and broke one of his ribs, and another man, by a fall, dislocated his shoulder. The gunner, who had the charge of a watch, was laid up with the rheumatism: and this was the first sick list that appeared on board the ship. The time of full moon, which was approaching, made me entertain hopes, that, after that period, we should experience some change of wind or weather in our favour; but the event did not at all answer our expectations. The latitude, at noon this day, was 58° 9′ S, and longitude 70° 1′ W.

As we caught a good many birds, but which were all lean, and tasted fishy, we tried an experiment upon them which succeeded admirably. By keeping them cooped up, and cramming them with ground corn, they improved wonderfully in a short time; so that the pintada birds became as fine as ducks, and the albatrosses were as fat, and not inferior in taste to fine geese. Some of the latter birds were caught that measured seven feet between the extremities of the wings, when spread. This unexpected supply came very opportunely; for none of our live stock remained except hogs, the sheep and poultry not being hardy enough to stand the severity of the weather.

This morning, the wind died away, and we had a calm for a few hours, which gave us hopes that the next would be a more favourable wind. A hog was killed for the ship's company, which gave them an excellent meal. Towards noon, to our great disappointment, the wind sprung up again from the westward, and in the afternoon blew strong, with snow and hail storms.

This was the second day after the full moon; but, as I have remarked before, it had no influence on the weather. At noon our latitude was 58° 31' S., and longitude 70° 7' W., which is near seven degrees to the eastward of our situation on the morning of the ninth instant, when we had advanced the farthest in our power to the westward, being then in 76° 58' W., three degrees to the west of Cape Deseada, the west part of the Straits of Magellan; and at this time we were 3° 52' to the east of it, and hourly losing ground.

It was with much concern I saw how hopeless, and even unjustifiable it was, to persist any longer in attempting a passage this way to the Society Islands. We had been thirty days in this tempestuous ocean. At one time we had advanced so far to the westward as to have a fair prospect of making our passage round; but from that period hard gales of westerly wind had continued without intermission, a few hours excepted, which, to borrow an expression in Lord Anson's voyage, were "like the elements drawing breath to return upon us with redoubled violence." The season was now too far advanced for us to expect more favourable winds or weather, and we had sufficiently experienced the impossibility of beating round against the wind, or of advancing at all without the help of a fair wind, for which there was little reason to hope. Another consideration, which had great weight with me, was, that if I persisted in my attempt this way, and should, after all, fail to get round, it would occasion such a loss of time, that our arrival at Otaheite, soon enough to return in the proper season by the East Indies, would be rendered precarious. On the other hand, the prevalence of the westerly winds in high southern latitudes, left me no reason to doubt of making a quick passage to the Cape of Good Hope, and thence to the eastward round New Holland. Having maturely considered all circumstances, I determined to bear away for the Cape of Good Hope; and at five o'clock on the evening of the 22d, the wind then blowing strong at west, I ordered the helm to be put a-weather, to the great joy of every person on board. Our sick list at this time had increased to eight, mostly with rheumatic complaints: in other respects the people were in good health, though exceedingly jaded.

The passage round Cape Horn, into the South Seas, during the summer months, has seldom been attended with difficulty, and is to be preferred, in the moderate seasons, to the more distant route to the eastward, round the Cape of Good Hope and New Holland. If we had been one month earlier, or perhaps less, I doubt not but we should have effected our passage.

CHAPTER III.

PASSAGE TOWARDS THE CAPE OF GOOD HOPE—ARRIVAL AT FALSE BAY—OCCURRENCES THERE—REPORTS CONCERNING THE GROSVENOR'S PEOPLE—DEPARTURE FROM THE CAPE.

THE westerly winds and stormy weather continuing, gave me no reason to repent of my determination. On the 25th at noon, we were in latitude 54° 16' S., and longitude 57° 4' W. The nearest of the Falkland Islands, by my reckoning, then bore N. 13° W.; distance 23 leagues. Our stock of water being sufficient to serve us to the Cape of Good Hope, I did not think it worth while to stop at those islands, as the refreshment we might obtain there would scarce repay us for the expense of time: we therefore continued our course towards the N.E. and E.N.E.

Thursday 22, at two in the afternoon, we saw the Table Mountain of the Cape of Good Hope. As it is reckoned unsafe riding in Table Bay at this time of the year, I steered for False Bay. The next evening we anchored in the outer part, and on the forenoon of the 24th got the ship secured in Simon's Bay, which is in the inner part of False Bay. We found lying here, one outward-bound Dutch Indiaman, five other Dutch ships, and a French ship.

After saluting the fort, which was returned by an equal number of guns, I went on shore, and dispatches were sent away to Cape Town, to acquaint the governor of our arrival. A Dutch ship at this time lying in Table Bay, bound for Europe, I sent letters by her to the Admiralty. It is very unusual for ships to be in Table Bay so late in the year, on account of the strong N.W. winds. April is the time limited.

I gave the necessary directions for getting our wants supplied. The ship required to be caulked in every part, for she was become so leaky, that we had been obliged to pump every hour in our passage from Cape Horn. This we immediately set about, as well as repairing our sails and rigging. The severe weather we had met with, and the leakiness of the ship, made it necessary to examine into the state of all the stores and provisions. Of the latter, a good deal was found damaged, particularly the bread.—The time-keeper I took on shore to ascertain its rate, and other instruments, to make the necessary astronomical observations. —Fresh meat, with soft bread, and plenty of vegetables, were issued daily to the ship's company, the whole time we remained here. A few days after our arrival, I went over to Cape Town, and waited on his excellency M. Vander Graaf, the governor, who obligingly arranged matters so much to our advantage, that we scarcely felt the inconvenience of being at a distance from the Cape Town, whence we received all our supplies.

During our stay here, I took care to procure seeds and plants that would be valuable at Otaheite, and the different places we might touch at in our way thither. In this I was greatly assisted by Colonel Gordon, the commander of the troops. In company with this gentleman, the loss of the Grosvenor East Indiaman was mentioned: on this subject, Colonel Gordon expressed great concern, that, from anything he had said, hopes were still entertained to flatter the affectionate wishes of the surviving friends of those unfortunate people. He said that, in his travels into the Caffre country, he had met with a native who described to him, that there was a white woman among his countrymen, who had a child, and that she frequently embraced the child, and cried most violently. This was all he (the colonel) could understand; and, being then on his return home, with his health much impaired by fatigue, the only thing that he could do, was to make a friend of the native, by presents, and promises of reward, on condition that he would take a letter to this woman, and bring him back an answer. Accordingly he wrote letters in English, French, and Dutch, desiring, that some sign or mark might be returned, either by writing with a burnt stick, or by any means she should be able to devise, to satisfy him that she was there; and that on receiving such token from her, every effort should be made to ensure her safety and escape. But the Caffre, although apparently delighted with the commission which he had undertaken, never returned, nor has the colonel ever heard any thing more of him, though he had been instructed in methods of conveying information through the Hottentot country.

To this account, that I may not again have occasion to introduce so melancholy a subject, I shall add the little information I received respecting it, when I re-visited the Cape, in my return towards Europe.—A reputable farmer, of the name of Holhousen, who lives at Swellendham, eight days' journey from the Cape, had information from some Caffre Hottentots, that at a crawl, or village, in their country, there were white men and women. On this intelligence, Mr. Holhousen asked permission of the governor to make an expedition, with some of the farmers, into the country, requiring a thousand rix-dollars to bear his expenses. The governor referred him to Mr. Wocke, the landros of Graverennet, a new colony, in his way. But from the place where Mr. Holhousen lives, to the landros Mr. Wocke's residence, is a month's journey, which he did not choose to undertake at an uncertainty, as Mr. Wocke might have disapproved of the enterprise. It was in October last that Mr. Holhousen offered to go on this service. He was one of the party who went along the sea-coast in search of these unfortunate people, when a few of them first made their appearance at the Cape. I am, however, informed, that the Dutch farmers are fond of making expeditions into the country, that they may have opportunities of taking away cattle; and this, I apprehend, to be one of the chief reasons why undertakings of this kind are not encouraged.

On the 13th of June, the Dublin East Indiaman arrived from England; on board of which ship was a party of the 77th regiment, under the command of Colonel Balfour.

On the 29th, being ready for sea, I took the time-keeper and instruments on board. The error of the time-keeper was 3' 33", 2 too slow for the mean time at Greenwich, and its rate of going 3" per day, losing. The thermometer, during our stay here, was from 51 to 66 degrees.

We had been thirty-eight days at this place, and my people had received all the advantage that could be derived from the refreshments of every kind that are here to be met with. We sailed at four o'clock this afternoon, and saluted the platform with thirteen guns as we ran out of the bay, which were returned.

CHAPTER IV.

PASSAGE TOWARDS VAN DIEMEN'S LAND—MAKE THE ISLAND OF ST. PAUL—ARRIVAL IN ADVENTURE BAY—NATIVES SEEN—SAIL FROM VAN DIEMEN'S LAND.

WE lost sight of the land the day after leaving False Bay, and steered towards the E.S.E., having variable winds the first week, with much thunder, lightning, and rain. The remainder of this passage, the winds were mostly between the S. and W., blowing strong. There were almost every day great numbers of pintada, albatrosses, blue petterels, and other oceanic birds, about us; but it was observed, that if the wind came from the northward, only for a few hours, the birds generally left us, and their presence again was the forerunner of a southerly wind.

On Sunday the 22nd, at noon, we were scudding under the fore-sail and close-reefed main-top-sail, the wind blowing strong from the west. An hour afternoon the gale increased, and blew with so much violence, that the ship was almost driven forecastle under, before we could get the sails clewed up. As soon as the sails were taken in, we brought the ship to the wind, lowered the lower yards, and got the top-gallant-masts upon deck, which eased the ship very much. We remained lying to till eight the next morning, when we bore away under a reefed fore-sail. In the afternoon the sea ran so high, that it became very unsafe to stand on: we therefore brought to the wind again, and remained lying to all night, without accident, excepting that the man at the steerage was thrown over the wheel, and much bruised. Towards noon, the violence of the storm abated, and we again bore away under the reefed fore-sail. In the afternoon saw some whales.

We continued running to the eastward, it being my intention to make the island St. Paul. On Monday the 28th, at six in the morning, we saw the island, bearing E. by N., 12 leagues distant; between 10 and 11 o'clock, we ran along the south side, at about a league distant from the shore. There was a verdure that covered the higher parts of the land; but I believe it was nothing more than moss, which is commonly found on the tops of most rocky islands in these latitudes. We saw several whales near the shore. The extent of this island is five miles from E. to W.; and about two or three from N. to S. As we passed the east end, we saw a remarkable high sugar-loaf rock, abreast of which, I have been informed, is good anchorage in 23 fathoms, the east point bearing S.W. by S., by true compass. I had this information from the captain of a Dutch packet, in which I returned to Europe. He likewise said there was good fresh water on the island, and a hot spring, which boiled fish in as great perfection as on a fire.

At noon, we were three leagues past the island. We kept on towards the E.S.E., and for several days continued to see rock-weed, which is remarked to be generally the case after ships pass St. Paul's; but to the westward of it, very seldom any is seen.

We had much bad weather, with snow and hail, and in our approach to Van Diemen's Land, nothing was seen to indicate the nearness of the coast, except a seal, when we were within the distance of 20 leagues.

At two o'clock this afternoon, we saw the rock named the Mewstone, that lies near the S.W. cape of Van Diemen's Land, bearing N.E. about six leagues. The wind blew strong from the N.W. As soon as we had passed the Mewstone, we were sheltered from a very heavy sea, which ran from the westward. At eight o'clock at night we were abreast of the south cape, when the wind became light and variable. Saw several fires inland.

All the 20th, we were endeavouring to get into Adventure Bay, but were prevented by variable winds. The next morning, at five o'clock, we anchored in the outer part, and at sun-rise weighed again: at noon, we anchored well in the bay, and moored the ship.

In our passage from the Cape of Good Hope, the winds were mostly from the westward, with very boisterous weather: but one great advantage, that this season of the year has over the summer months is, in being free from fogs. I have already remarked, that the approach of strong southerly winds is announced by many kinds of birds of the albatross or petterel tribe, and the abatement of the gale, or a shift of wind to the northward, by their keeping away. The thermometer also very quickly shows when a change of these winds may be expected, by varying sometimes six and seven degrees in its height. I have reason to believe, that after we passed the island St. Paul, there was a westerly current; the ship being every day to the westward of the reckoning, which in the whole, from St. Paul to Van Diemen's Land, made a difference of four degrees between the longitude by the reckoning and the true longitude.

The ship being moored, I went in a boat to look out for the most convenient place to wood and water at, which I found to be at the west end of the beach: for the surf, though considerable, was less there than at any other part of the bay. The water was in a gully about sixty yards from the beach; it was perfectly good, but being only a collection from the rains, the place is always dry in the summer months; for we found no water in it when I was here with Captain Cook in January, 1777.—We had very little success in hauling the seine: about twenty small flounders, and flatheaded fish, called foxes, were all that were taken.

I found no signs of the natives having lately frequented this bay, or of any European vessels having been here since the Resolution and Discovery in 1777. From some of the old trunks of trees, then cut down, I saw shoots about twenty-five feet high, and fourteen inches in circumference.

In the evening, I returned on board. The next morning, 22nd, at daylight, a party was sent on shore for wooding and watering, under the command of Mr. Christian and the gunner; and I directed that one man should be constantly employed in washing the people's clothes. There was so much surf that the wood was obliged to be rafted off in bundles to the boat. Mr. Nelson informed me, that, in his walks to-day, he saw a tree, in a very healthy state, which he measured, and found to be thirty-three feet and a half in girth; its height was proportioned to its bulk.

Saturday the 23rd. The surf was rather greater than yesterday, which very much interrupted our wooding and watering. Nelson to-day picked up a male opossum that had been recently killed, or had died, for we could not perceive any wound, unless it had received a blow on the back, where there was a bare place about the size of a shilling. It measured fourteen inches from the ears to the beginning of the tail, which was exactly the same length.

Most of the forest trees were at this time shedding their bark. There are three kinds, which are distinguished from each other by their leaves, though the wood appears to be the same. Many of them are full one hundred and fifty feet high; but most of those that we cut down, were decayed at the heart. There are, besides the forest trees, several other kinds that are firm good wood, and may be cut for most purposes, except masts; neither are the forest trees good for masts, on account of their weight, and the difficulty of finding them thoroughly sound. Mr. Nelson asserted that they shed their bark every year, and that they increase more from the seed than by suckers.

I found the tide made a difference of full two feet in the height of the water in the lake, at the back of the beach. At high water, it was very brackish, but at low tide, it was perfectly fresh to the taste, and soap showed no sign of its being the least impregnated. We had better success in fishing on board the ship, than by hauling the seine on shore; for, with hooks and lines, a number of fine rock cod were caught.—I saw to-day several eagles, some beautiful blue-plumaged herons, and a great variety of paroquets. A few oyster-catchers and gulls were generally about the beach, and in the lake a few wild ducks.

Being in want of plank, I directed a saw-pit to be dug, and employed some of the people to saw trees into plank. The greater part of this week the winds were moderate, with unsettled weather. On Friday it blew strong from the S.W., with rain, thunder, and lightning. We continued to catch fish in sufficient quantities for every body, and had better success with the seine.—We were fortunate, also, in angling in the lake, where we caught some very fine tench. Some of the people felt a sickness from eating muscles, that were gathered from the rocks; but I believe it was occasioned by eating too many. We found some spider-crabs, most of them not good, being the female sort, and out of season. The males were tolerably good, and were known by the smallness of their two fore-claws, or feeders. We saw the trunk of a dead tree, on which had been cut "A. D. 1773." The figures were very distinct; even the slips made with the knife were discernible. This must have been done by some of captain Furneaux's people, in March, 1773, fifteen years before. The marks of the knife remaining so unaltered, I imagine the tree must have been dead when it was cut; but it serves to show the durability of the wood, for it was perfectly sound at this time. I shot two gannets; these birds were of the same size as those in England; their colour is a beautiful white, with the wings and tail tipped with jet black, and the top and back of the head of a very fine yellow. Their feet were black, with four claws, on each of which was a yellow line, the whole length of the foot. The bill was four inches long, without nostrils, and very taper and sharp-pointed.

The east side of the bay being not so thick of wood as the other parts, and the soil being good, I fixed on it, at Nelson's recommendation, as the most proper situation for planting some of the fruit-trees which I had brought from the Cape of Good Hope. A circumstance much against any thing succeeding here, is, that in the dry season, the fires made by the natives are apt to communicate to the dried grass and underwood, and to spread in such a manner as to endanger every thing that cannot bear a severe scorching. We, however, chose what we thought the safest situations, and planted three fine young apple-trees, nine vines, six plantain-trees, a number of orange and lemon-seed, cherry-stones, plum, peach, and apricot-stones, pumpkins, also two sorts of Indian corn, and apple and pear kernels. The ground is well adapted for the trees, being of a rich loamy nature. The spot where we made our plantation was clear of underwood; and we marked the trees that stood nearest to the different things which were planted. Nelson followed the circuit of the bay, planting in such places as appeared most eligible. I have great hopes that some of these articles will succeed. The particular situations I had described in my survey of this place, but I was unfortunately prevented from bringing it home. Near the watering place, likewise, we planted on a flat, which appeared a favourable situation, some onions, cabbage-roots, and potatoes.

For some days past, a number of whales were seen in the bay. They were of the same kind as those we had generally met with before, having two blow-holes on the back of the head.

On the night of the 1st of September, we observed, for the first time, signs of the natives being in the neighbourhood. Fires were seen on the low land, near Cape Frederick Henry, and at daylight, we saw the natives with our glasses. As I expected they would come round to us, I remained all the forenoon near the wooding and watering parties, making observations, the morning being very favourable for that purpose. I was, however, disappointed in my conjecture, for the natives did not appear, and there was too great a surf for a boat to land on the part where we had seen them.

The natives not coming near us, I determined, on the 2nd, to go after them, and we set out, in a boat, towards Cape Frederick Henry, where we arrived about eleven o'clock. I found landing impracticable, and therefore came to a grapnel, in hopes of their coming to us, for we had passed several fires. After waiting near an hour, I was surprised to see Nelson's assistant come out of the wood: he had wandered thus far in search of plants, and told me that he had met with some of the natives. Soon after we heard their voices like the cackling of geese, and twenty persons came out of the wood, twelve of whom went round to some rocks, where the boat could get nearer to the shore than we then were. Those who remained behind were women.

We approached within twenty yards of them, but there was no possibility of landing, and I could only throw to the shore, tied up in paper, the presents which I intended for them. I showed the different articles as I tied them up, but they would not untie the paper till I made an appearance of leaving them. They then opened the parcels, and, as they took the articles out, placed them on their heads. On seeing this, I returned towards them, when they instantly put every thing out of their hands, and would not appear to take notice of any thing that we had given them. After throwing a few more beads and nails on shore, I made signs for them to go to the ship, and they, likewise, made signs for me to land; but as this could not be effected, I left them, in hopes of a nearer interview at the watering place.

When they first came in sight, they made a prodigious clattering in their speech, and held their arms over their heads. They spoke so quick, that I could not catch one single word they uttered. We recollected one man, whom we had formerly seen among the party of the natives that came to us in 1777, and who is particularised in the account of Captain Cook's last voyage, for his humour and deformity. Some of them had a small stick, two or three feet long, in their hands, but no other weapon.

Their colour, as Captain Cook remarks, is a dull black; their skin is scarified about their shoulders and breast. They were of a middle stature, or rather below it. One of them was distinguished by his body being coloured with red ochre, but all the others were painted black, with a kind of soot, which was laid on so thick over their faces and shoulders, that it is difficult to say what they were like.

They ran very nimbly over the rocks, had a very quick sight, and caught the small beads and nails, which I threw to them, with great dexterity. They talked to us sitting on their heels, with their knees close into their armpits, and were perfectly naked.

In my return towards the ship, I landed at the point of the harbour near Penguin Island, and from the hills, saw the water on the other side of the low isthmus of Cape Frederick Henry, which forms the bay of that name. It is very extensive, and in, or near, the middle of the bay, there is a low island. From this spot, it has the appearance of being a very good and convenient harbour.

The account which I had from Brown, the botanist's assistant, was, that in his search for plants, he had met an old man, a young woman, and two or three children. The old man at first appeared alarmed, but became familiar on being presented with a knife. He nevertheless sent away the young woman, who went very reluctantly. He saw some miserable wigwams, in which were nothing but a few kangaroo skins spread on the ground, and a basket made of rushes.

Among the wood that we cut here, we found many scorpions and centipes, with numerous black ants that were an inch long. We saw no musquitos, though in the summer months they are very troublesome.

What is called the New Zealand tea plant, grew here in great abundance; so that it was not only gathered and dried to use as tea, but made excellent brooms. It bears a small pointed leaf, of a pleasant smell, and its seed is contained in a berry, about the size of a pea, notched into five equal parts on the top. The soil, on the west and south sides of the bay, is black mould, with a mixture of fine white sand, and is very rich. The trees are lofty and large, and the underwood grows so close together, that in many places it is impassable. The east side of the bay is a rich loamy soil; but, near the tops of the hills, is very much encumbered with stones and rocks: the underwood thinly placed and small. The trees on the S.S.E. and S.W. sides of the hills, grow to a larger size than those that are exposed to the opposite points; for the sides of the trees open or exposed to the north winds are naked, with few branches; while the other sides are in a flourishing state. From this I do not infer, that the equatorial are more hurtful than the polar winds; but that the trees, by their situation, were more sheltered from the one than from the other.

A calm prevented our sailing to-day. The friendly interview which we had had with the natives, made me expect that they would have paid us a visit; but we saw nothing more of them, except fires in the night, upon the low land to the northward.

This forenoon, having a pleasant breeze at N.W., we weighed anchor, and sailed out of Adventure Bay.

CHAPTER V.

ROCKY ISLANDS DISCOVERED—SEE THE ISLAND MAITEA, AND ARRIVE AT OTAHEITE—SHIP CROWDED BY THE NATIVES.

BEING clear of the land, we steered towards the E.S.E., it being my intention to pass to the southward of New Zealand, as I expected in that route to meet with constant westerly winds; in which, however, I was disappointed, for they proved variable, and frequently from the eastward blowing strong, with thick misty weather. The thermometer varied from 41 to 46 degrees.

On the 14th, at noon, we were in 49° 24′ S. latitude, and in 168° 3′ E. longitude, which is on the same meridian with the south end of New Zealand. We altered our course, steering to the northward of east, and frequently saw rock-weed, which I supposed to have drifted from New Zealand. The sea now became rougher, from our being exposed to a long swell, which came from the N. E.

On the 19th, at day-light, we discovered a cluster of small rocky islands, bearing east by north four leagues distant from us. We had seen no birds, or any thing to indicate the nearness of land, except patches of rock-weed, for which the vicinity of New Zealand sufficiently accounted. The wind being at N.E. prevented our near approach to these isles; so that we were not less than three leagues distant in passing to the southward of them. The weather was too thick to see distinctly: their extent was only three and a half miles from east to west, and about half a league from north to south: their number, including the smaller ones, was thirteen. I could not observe any verdure on any of them: there were white spots like patches of snow; but, as Captain Cook, in describing the land of New Zealand, near Cape South, says, in many places there are patches like white marble, it is probable that what we saw might be of the same kind as what he had observed. The westernmost of those islands is the largest; they are of sufficient height to be seen at the distance of seven leagues from a ship's deck. While in sight of the islands, we saw some penguins, and a white kind of gull with a forked tail. Captain Cook's track, in 1773, was near this spot, but he did not see the islands: he saw seals and penguins hereabouts, but considered New Zealand to be the nearest land. I have named them after the ship, the Bounty Isles.

On Sunday, the 21st, we saw a seal, some rockweed, and a great many albatrosses.

October 2nd, Thursday, it being calm, and a number of small blubbers about the ship, I took up some in a bucket, but I saw no difference between them and the common blubbers in the West Indies. We frequently, in the night-time, observed the sea to be covered with luminous spots, caused by prodigious quantities of small blubbers, that, from the strings which extend from them, emit a light like the blaze of a candle, while the body continues perfectly dark.

The 3rd, in the morning, we saw a seal. Captain Cook has remarked seeing sea-weed, when nearly in the same place. Our latitude 40° 21′ S., longitude 215° E. Being now well to the eastward of the Society Islands, I steered more to the northward.

We continued to have the southern oceanic birds accompany us, and a few whales. The people caught albatrosses, and fattened them in the same manner which they had done when off Cape Horn. Some of these measured near eight feet between the tips of the wings, when spread.

On Thursday, the 9th, we had the misfortune to lose one of our seamen, James Valentine, who died in the night, of an asthmatic complaint. This poor man had been one of the most robust people on board, until our arrival at Adventure Bay, where he first complained of some slight indisposition, for which he was bled, and got better. Some time afterwards, the arm in which he had been bled, became painful and inflamed; the inflammation increased, with a hollow cough, and extreme difficulty of breathing, to his death.

The 13th, in the afternoon, we saw two land birds, like what are called sand-larks. Our latitude at this time was 28° 3′ S., and longitude 223° 26′ E. The next morning we saw a tropic bird, and some fish. The winds were light and variable, with calms, from this time to the 19th, when a breeze sprung up from the N.E., which gradually came round to the eastward, and proved to be the trade wind.

On the 25th, at half past seven in the morning, we saw the Island Maitea, called Osnaburg by Captain Wallis, who first discovered it. As Captain Wallis and Captain Cook had both passed near the south side, I ran along the north side, which is remarkably steep. The island is high and round, and not more than three miles in its greatest extent. The south side, where the declivity from the hill is more gradual, is the chief place of residence of the natives; but the north side, from the very summit down to the sea, is so steep, that it can afford no support to the inhahitants. We steered pretty close in to the north-ward of the east end, where we saw but few habi-tations; a very neat house on a small eminence, delightfully situated in a grove of cocoa-nut-trees, particularly attracted our notice. About twenty of the natives followed us along shore, waving and showing large pieces of cloth; but the surf on the shore was too high to think of having any communication with them. I observed a great number of cocoa-nut-trees, but did not see one plantain-tree. There were other trees, but of what kind we could not distinguish: near the east end are two remarkable rocks, and a reef runs off to the eastward about half a league.

We continued our course to the westward, and at six in the evening saw Otaheite, bearing W. ¼ S.; the island Maitea, then in sight, bearing E. ¼ S., eight leagues distant. As there was great probability that we should remain a considerable time at Otaheite, it could not be expected that the intercourse of my people with the natives should be of a very reserved nature: I therefore ordered that every person should be examined by the surgeon, and had the satisfaction to learn, from his report, that they were all perfectly free from any venereal complaint.

On the 26th, at four o'clock in the morning, having run twenty-five leagues from Maitea, we brought to till day-light, when we saw Point Venus bearing S.W. by W., distant about four leagues. As we drew near, a great number of canoes came off to us. Their first enquiries were, if we were *tyos*, which signifies friends; and whether we came from *Pretanie*, (their pronunciation of Britain) or from Lima: they were no sooner satisfied in this, than they crowded on board in vast numbers, notwithstanding our endeavours to prevent it, as we were working the ship in; and in less than ten minutes, the deck was so full that I could scarce find my own people. At nine in the forenoon, we were obliged to anchor in the outer part of Matavai Bay, in thirteen fathoms, being prevented by light variable winds from placing the ship in a proper birth.

This passage of fifty-two days from Van Diemen's land may be rated as moderate sailing. We passed New Zealand with the spring equinox, and the winds, though strong, were at no time violent. To the southward of 40° 0′ S. they were variable; between the latitudes of 40 and 33° S., the wind kept in the N.W. quarter; afterwards, till we got into the trade, the winds were variable, mostly from the eastward, but light, and inclinable to calms. The ship was 3° 22′ in longitude to the eastward of the dead reckoning, which the time-keeper almost invariably proved to be owing to a current giving us more easting than the log. Our track was as distant from any course of former ships as I could conveniently make it; and though we made no new discoveries, except the small cluster of islands near New Zealand, yet in other parts of the track, as has been noticed, we met with signs of being in the neighbourhood of land.

It may not be unworthy of remark, that the whole distance which the ship had run by the log, in direct and contrary courses, from leaving Eng-land to our anchoring at Otaheite, was twenty-seven thousand and eighty-six miles, which, on an average, is at the rate of a hundred and eight miles each twenty-four hours.

CHAPTER VI.

ACCOUNT OF AN ENGLISH SHIP LATELY SAILED FROM OTA-HEITE—DEATH OF OMAI—CAPTAIN COOK'S PICTURE SENT ON BOARD—OTOO VISITS THE SHIP—HIS VISIT RETURNED—NATIVES WELL DISPOSED TOWARDS US—ACCOUNT OF THE CATTLE LEFT BY CAPTAIN COOK—BREAD-FRUIT PLANTS PROMISED—VISIT TO THE EAREE DAHE—PRESENTS MADE TO THE ARREOYS.

THE ship being anchored, Sunday, 26th, our number of visitors continued to increase; but as yet we saw no person that we could recollect to have been of much consequence. Some inferior chiefs made me presents of a few hogs, and I made them presents in return. We were supplied with cocoa-nuts in great abundance, but bread-fruit was scarce.

Many inquiries were made after Captain Cook, Sir Joseph Banks, and many of their former friends. They said a ship had been here, from which they had learnt that Captain Cook was dead; but the circumstances of his death they did not appear to be acquainted with; and I had given particular directions to my officers and ship's company, that they should not be mentioned. The ship spoken of, they informed me, staid at Otaheite one month, and had been gone four months, by some of their accounts; according to others, only three months. The captain they called Tonah. I understood likewise from them, that Lieutenant Watts was in the ship; who, having been here in the Resolution with Captain Cook, was well known to them.—One of my first enquiries, as will naturally be imagined, was after our friend Omai *; and it was a sensible mortifi-cation and disappointment to me to hear that not only Omai, but both the New Zealand boys who had been left with him, were dead. Every one agreed in their information that they died a natural death. Otoo, who was the chief of Matavai when Captain Cook was here the last time, was absent at another part of the island; they told me mes-sengers were sent to inform him of our arrival, and that he was expected to return soon. There appeared among the natives in general great good-will towards us, and they seemed to be much rejoiced at our arrival. This whole day we expe-rienced no instance of dishonesty. We were so much crowded, that I could not undertake to remove to a more proper station, without danger of disobliging our visitors, by desiring them to leave the ship: this business was therefore de-ferred till the next morning.

Early in the morning of Monday, before the natives began to flock off to us, we weighed anchor, to work farther into the bay, and moored at about a quarter of a mile distance from the shore; the ship lying in seven fathoms water.

Several chiefs now came on board, and ex-pressed great pleasure at seeing me. Among these were Otow, the father of Otoo, and Oreepyah, his brother; also another chief of Matavai, called Poeeno: and to these men I made presents. Two messengers likewise arrived from Otoo, to acquaint me of his being on his way to the ship; each of whom brought me, as a present from Otoo, a small pig, and a young plantain-tree, as a token of

---

* Carried to England by Captain Cook.

friendship. The ship was now plentifully supplied with provisions; every person having as much as he could consume.

As soon as the ship was secured, I went on shore with the chief Poeeno, and accompanied by a multitude of the natives. He conducted me to the place where we had fixed our tents in 1777, and desired that I would now appropriate the spot to the same use. We then went across the beach, and through a walk delightfully shaded with bread-fruit trees, to his own house. Here we found two women at work staining a piece of cloth red. These I found were his wife and her sister. They desired me to sit down on a mat, which was spread for the purpose, and with great kindness offered me refreshments. I received the congratulations of several strangers, who came to us and behaved with great decorum and attention. The people, however, thronged about the house in such numbers, that I was much incommoded by the heat, which being observed, they immediately drew back. Among the crowd I saw a man who had lost his arm just above the elbow; the stump was well covered, and the cure seemed as perfect as could be expected from the greatest professional skill.

I made inquiries about the cattle that had been left here by Captain Cook, but the accounts I received were very unfavourable, and so various, that for the present I shall forbear speaking of them. After staying about an hour, I got up to take leave, when the women, in a very obliging manner, came to me with a mat, and a piece of their finest cloth, which they put on me after the Otaheite fashion. When I was thus dressed, they each of them took one of my hands, and accompanied me to the water-side, and at parting promised that they would soon return my visit.

In this walk I had the satisfaction to see that the island had received some benefit from our former visits. Two shaddocks were brought to me, a fruit which they had not till we introduced it; and among the articles which they brought off to the ship, and offered for sale, were capsicums, pumpkins, and two young goats.

On my return to the ship, I found that a small disturbance had been occasioned by one of the natives making an attempt to steal a tin pot; which, on being known to Oreepyah, he flew into a violent rage, and it was with some difficulty that the thief escaped with his life. He drove all his countrymen out of the ship; and when he saw me, he desired if at any time I found a thief, that I would order him to be tied up and punished with a severe flogging.

This forenoon a man came on board with Capt. Cook's picture, which had been drawn by Mr. Webber in 1777, and left with Otoo. It was brought to me to be repaired. The frame was broken, but the picture no way damaged, except a little in the back ground. They called it *Toote* (which has always been their manner of pronouncing Captain Cook's name) *Earee no Otaheite*, chief of Otaheite. They said Toote had desired Otoo, whenever any English ship came, to show the picture, and it would be acknowledged as a token of friendship. The youngest brother of Otoo, named Whydooah, visited me this afternoon: he appeared stupified with drinking ava. At sunset all our male visitors left the ship.

The next morning early I received a message from Otoo, to inform me of his arrival, and requesting that I would send a boat for him; which I immediately did, with an officer (Mr. Christian) to conduct him on board. He came with numerous attendants, and expressed much satisfaction at our meeting. After introducing his wife to me, we joined noses, the customary manner of saluting, and, to perpetuate our friendship, he desired we should exchange names. I was surprised to find that, instead of Otoo, the name by which he formerly went, he was now called Tinah. The name of Otoo, with the title of *Earee Rahie*, I was informed had devolved to his eldest son, who was yet a minor, as is the custom of the country. The name of Tinah's wife was Iddeah: with her was a woman, dressed with a large quantity of cloth, in the form of a hoop, which was taken off and presented to me, with a large hog, and some bread-fruit. I then took my visitors into the cabin, and after a short time produced my presents in return. The present I made to Tinah (by which name I shall hereafter call him) consisted of hatchets, small adzes, files, gimblets, saws, looking-glasses, red feathers, and two shirts. To Iddeah I gave ear-rings, necklaces, and beads; but she expressed a desire also for iron, and therefore I made the same assortment for her as I had for her husband. Much conversation took place among them on the value of the different articles, and they appeared extremely satisfied; so that they determined to spend the day with me, and requested I would show them all over the ship, and particularly the cabin where I slept. This, though I was not fond of doing, I indulged them in, and the consequence was, as I had apprehended, that they took a fancy to so many things, that they got from me nearly as much more as I had before given them. Afterwards, Tinah desired me to fire some of the great guns: this I likewise complied with, and, as the shot fell into the sea at a great distance, all the natives expressed their surprise by loud shouts and acclamations.

I had a large company at dinner; for, besides Tinah and his wife, there was Otow, the father of Tinah, Oreepyah, and Whydooah, two of his brothers, Poeeno, and several other chiefs. Tinah was a very large man, much above the common stature, being not less than six feet four inches in height, and proportionably stout: his age about thirty-five. His wife (Iddeah) I judged to be about twenty-four years of age: she was likewise much above the common size of the women at Otaheite, and had a very animated and intelligent countenance. Whydooah, the younger brother of Tinah, was highly spoken of as a warrior, but had the character of being the greatest drunkard in the country; and, indeed, to judge from the withered appearance of his skin, he must have used the pernicious drink called ava, to great excess. Tinah was fed by one of his attendants, who sat by him for that purpose, this being a particular custom among some of the superior chiefs; and I must do him the justice to say, he kept his attendant constantly employed: there was indeed little reason to complain of want of appetite in any of my guests. As the women are not allowed to eat in presence of the men, Iddeah dined with some of her companions about an hour afterwards, in private, except that her husband Tinah favoured them with his company, and seemed to have entirely forgotten that he had already dined.

Provisions were brought off to the ship in the greatest plenty; and, to prevent as much as possible anything which might occasion disputes, I desired Mr. Peckover, the gunner, to undertake the management of our traffic with the natives. Some of the hogs brought to-day weighed 200 lbs., and we purchased several for salting. Goats were likewise brought off for sale, and I bought a she-goat and kid for less than would have purchased a small hog. Our friends here expressed much disappointment that there was no portrait painter on board; Tinah in particular, who wished to have had pictures of his father and family.

An intimacy between the natives and our people was already so general, that there was scarce a man in the ship who had not his *tyo* or friend. Tinah continued with me the whole afternoon, in the course of which he ate four times of roast pork, besides his dinner. When he left the ship, he requested I would keep for him all the presents I had given to him, as he had not, at Matavai, a place sufficiently safe to secure them from being stolen; I therefore showed him a locker in my cabin for his use, and gave him a key to it. This is perhaps not so much a proof of his want of power, as of the estimation in which they hold European commodities, and which makes more than the common means of security necessary to prevent theft.

I had sent Nelson and his assistant to look for plants, and it was no small pleasure to me to find, by their report, that, according to appearances, the object of my mission would probably be accomplished with ease. I had given directions to every one on board not to make known to the islanders the purpose of our coming, lest it might enhance the value of the bread-fruit plants, or occasion other difficulties. Perhaps so much caution was not necessary; but at all events I wished to reserve to myself the time and manner of communication. Nelson met with two fine shaddock-trees, which he had planted in 1777: they were full of fruit, but not ripe.

Wednesday, 29th.—In the morning I returned Tinah's visit, for I found he expected it. He was in a small shed about a quarter of a mile to the eastward of Matavai Point, with his wife and three children, not their own, but who they said were relations. In my walk I had picked up a numerous attendance, for every one I met followed me; so that I had collected such a crowd that the heat was scarce bearable, every one endeavouring to get a look to satisfy their curiosity; they, however, carefully avoided pressing against me, and welcomed me with cheerful countenances, and great good-nature.

I made Tinah understand that my visit was particularly to him, and gave him a second present, equal to the first, which he received with great pleasure; and to the people of consequence that were about him I also presented some article or other. There were great numbers of children; and, as I took notice of the little ones that were in arms, and gave them beads, both small and great, but with much drollery and good-humour, endeavoured to benefit by the occasion. Boys of ten and twelve years old were caught up in arms and brought to me, which created much laughter; so

that in a short time I got rid of all I had brought on shore.

In my return I called on Poeeno and an elderly chief, a relation of his, called Moannah, the principal men of this district, and with whom I judged it my interest to be on good terms. I gave them several valuable articles; and as the situation here was eligible for a garden, I planted melon, cucumber, and salad-seeds. I told them many other things should be sown for their use; and they appeared much pleased when they understood I intended to plant such things as would grow to be trees and produce fruit. I saw large patches of tobacco growing without culture, and many pumpkin vines. The bread-fruit trees and cocoa-nut trees at this time were full of fruit.

I went on board to dinner, and Moannah accompanied me. In the afternoon I returned to Poeeno's, with some additional seeds to improve the little garden I had begun to make in the forenoon. While I was giving directions, I received a message from Tinah, inviting me to come to him at his brother Oreepyah's house, which was near the beach. At this place I found a great number of people collected, who, on my appearance, immediately made way for me to sit down by Tinah. The crowd being ordered to draw back, a piece of cloth about two yards wide and forty-one yards in length was spread on the ground; and another piece of cloth was brought by Oreepyah, which he put over my shoulders and round my waist, in the manner the chiefs are clothed. Two large hogs, weighing each above two hundred pounds, and a quantity of baked bread-fruit and cocoa-nuts, were then laid before me, as a present, and I was desired to walk from one end of the cloth spread on the ground to the other, in the course of which, Tyo and Ehoah * were repeated with loud acclamations. This ceremony being ended, Tinah desired I would send the things on board, which completely loaded the boat; we therefore waited till she came back, and then I took them on board with me; for I knew they expected some return. The present which I made on this occasion was equal to any that I had made before; but I discovered that Tinah was not the sole proprietor of what he had given to me, for the present I gave was divided among those who I guessed had contributed to support his dignity; among whom were Moannah, Poeeno, and Oreepyah; Tinah, however, kept the greatest part of what I had given, and every one seemed satisfied with the proportion he allotted them.

The Otaheite breed of hogs seems to be supplanted by the European. Originally they were of the China sort, short, and very thick-necked; but the superior size of the European has made them encourage our breed.

Thursday, 30th.—At break of day, Tinah and his wife came again to the ship, and as their attendants were numerous, I provided a breakfast for them of broiled and roasted pork, which they preferred to tea. Our arrival being known all over the island, we had this day a great number of strangers on board, who came from the most remote parts, and in the forenoon some hooks and thimbles were cut out from the blocks. This induced me to order all the natives out of the ship, except

---

* Tyo and Ehoah are words of the same signification; i.e. *friend.*

the chiefs and their attendants. In executing these orders, a daring fellow attacked the sentinel, but escaped among the crowd. Every one knew the consequence of offending the sentinel, and were exceedingly alarmed at the appearance of anger I thought necessary to assume.

Among those who visited us to-day were two chiefs of great consequence, Marrowarre and his son Poohaitaiah Otee, Earees of the districts of Itteeah and Attahooroo. Otee was fed at dinner in the same manner as Tinah. It was evident that the attention which I showed to these chiefs seemed to give uneasiness to Tinah. At sunset my visitors took leave, and were carried on shore by one of the ship's boats, which has always been regarded as a mark of distinction, and on that account preferred by them to going in their own canoes. At their request a race was rowed between our five-oared cutter and one of their double canoes with four paddles. Great exertions were used on both sides, but the cutter first reached the shore. In their return to the ship, Oreopyah stopped them, till a large piece of cloth that he had sent for was brought, which he tied to the boat-hook, and desired should be carried off as a trophy of their victory.

The next morning, at sunrise, Moannah came on board with a message from Tinah, to acquaint me that he was *matow* (afraid to see me) till he had recovered some things that had been stolen from the ship, and which he had sent after. I knew there was something wrong, as no canoes came off to us, and, on looking about, we found the buoy of the best bower anchor had been taken away, I imagine, for the sake of some iron hoops that were on it. That this might not create any coolness, I sent a boat to Tinah, to invite him and his friends to come on board; which they immediately did, and were no longer under any apprehensions. I had made an appointment with Oreopyah, for him to go with me to Oparre this morning; but the accident just mentioned caused him to break his engagement, he having gone, I was informed, in search of what had been stolen.

Oparre is the district next to the westward of Matavai. One of my reasons for going to Oparre, was to see if Nelson would be able to procure plants there; but I gave the credit of my visit to young Otoo, the son of Tinah, who was the Earee Rahie, and lived with the rest of Tinah's children at Oparre. I prepared a magnificent present for this youth, who was represented to me as the person of the greatest consequence, or rather of the highest rank, in the island. At noon I left the ship, accompanied by Tinah, his wife Iddeah, and Poeeno. Moannah was to have been of the party, but he insisted on remaining in the ship, to prevent his countrymen from attempting to steal anything.

After half an hour's sailing, we arrived at Oparre. During this time, Tinah gave me a more circumstantial account of the cattle and sheep, that had been left with him: he related, that after five years from the time of Captain Cook's departure (counting sixty-three moons) the people of the island Eimeo joined with those of Attahooroo, a district of Otaheite, and made a descent on Oparre: that after some resistance, by which many men were killed, Tinah and his people fled to the mountains, leaving all their property to the mercy of the victorious party, who destroyed almost every thing which they found not convenient to take

away with them. Some of the cattle were killed and eaten, but the greater part were taken to Eimeo. The cows, he said, had produced eight calves, and the ewes ten young ones. The ducks, among which they classed the geese, had greatly increased; but the turkeys and peacocks, whatever was the cause, had not bred. It seemed to give Tinah great pleasure to observe how much I was concerned for the destruction of so many useful animals; but the cause of his satisfaction, I found, did not proceed from any expectation that I should replace them, but from the belief that I would take vengeance on the people who had deprived him of them; for with respect to the loss of the cattle, he appeared so unconcerned and indifferent, that I was very angry with him. There is, however, sufficient excuse for his resentment against the people of Eimeo; for the large extensive houses, which we had seen in this part of Otaheite, in the year 1777, were all destroyed, and at present they had no other habitations than light sheds, which might be taken by the four corners, and removed by four men; and of the many large canoes which they then had, not more than three remained. Tinah, understanding from my conversation, that I intended visiting some of the other islands in this neighbourhood, very earnestly desired I would not think of leaving Matavai. "Here," said he, "you shall be supplied plentifully with every thing you want. All here are your friends, and friends of king George: if you go to the other islands, you will have every thing stolen from you." I replied, that on account of their good-will, and from a desire to serve him and his country, King George had sent out those valuable presents to him; "and will not you, Tinah, send something to King George in return?"—"Yes," he said, "I will send him any thing I have;" and then began to enumerate the different articles in his power, among which he mentioned the bread-fruit. This was the exact point to which I wished to bring the conversation; and, seizing an opportunity, which had every appearance of being undesigned and accidental, I told him the bread-fruit trees were what King George would like; upon which he promised me a great many should be put on board, and seemed much delighted to find it so easily in his power to send any thing that would be well received by King George.

On landing at Oparre, an immense crowd of natives, as usual, immediately thronged about us. I inquired for Oreopyah, whom I expected to have met me here, but he was not yet returned from his search after the thieves; we therefore went under a shed of his to wait for him, and in about a quarter of an hour he joined us, bringing with him an iron scraper, and one of the hoops of the buoy. I thanked him for the trouble which he had taken, and assured him that I was perfectly satisfied; for he still seemed apprehensive of my displeasure.

We took leave, for a short time, of Oreopyah, and I proceeded with Tinah to make my visit to the young Otoo, the *Earee Rahie*. When we had walked about five minutes, Tinah stopped, and informed me that no person could be permitted to see his son, who was covered above the shoulders. He then took off his upper garments, and requested I would do the same. I replied, that I had no objection to go as I would to my own king, who was the greatest in all the world; and pulling off my hat, he threw a piece of cloth round my shoulders, and we went on. About a quarter of a mile farther towards the hills, through a delightful shade of bread-fruit trees, we stopped at the side of a small serpentine river: here I was in view of a house on the other side, at about fifty yards distance. From this house the young king was brought out on a man's shoulders, clothed in a piece of fine white cloth, and I was desired by Tinah to salute him by the name of *Too Earee Rahie*. The present which I had prepared was divided into three parts, and two other children made their appearance in the same manner. The first present I gave to a messenger who attended for that purpose; and I was instructed by Tinah to say, that it was for the *Earee Rahie*; that I was his friend; that I hated thieves; and that I came from Britannia. The second present was sent in the same manner, with a similar message, to one of the other children; and likewise the third.

As I could not see the *Earee Rahie* distinctly, I desired to be permitted to go over the river to him; but this, it seems, could not be complied with: therefore, after seeing the presents delivered, I returned with Tinah towards Oreepyah's house. I was informed that Tinah had four children by his wife, Iddeah. Otoo, or Too, the *Earee Rahie*, appeared to be about six years old: the second is a girl, named Terreeah Oroah; the third, a boy, Terreetappanooai; and a fourth, an infant girl, whom I did not see, named Tahamydooah.

When we came to the place where we had first stopped, Tinah took the cloth from my shoulders, and desired me to put my hat on; I expressed a desire to see more of the place, and he took me back by a different way. On passing a trunk of a tree, rudely carved, I was desired again to pull my hat off, and all uncovered their shoulders. This I discovered to be nothing more than the boundary of the king's land; on which, whoever set their feet, uncovered themselves out of respect.

We stopped at a house belonging to Tinah, where I was treated with a concert of one drum and three flutes, with singing by four men. I made some presents to the performers, and we removed to Oreepyah's house, where, after paying my compliments to him, which I found was expected, Tinah made me a present of a large hog, and some cocoa-nuts. He then introduced an uncle of his, called Mowworoah, a very old man, much tattooed, and almost blind. To this chief I made a present; and soon after I embarked, with Tinah, Oreepyah, their wives, and Poeeno. A vast number of people were collected on the beach to see us depart; and as soon as the boat had put off, Tinah desired me to fire my pocket-pistol, the *poopooe oie eie*, as he called it: the report seemed to electrify the whole crowd; but finding no harm done, they gave great shouts of approbation.

Nelson, who accompanied me in this expedition, had but little opportunity to search after plants, the natives having crowded so much about him: he saw enough, however, to assure him that they were to be procured here as plentifully as at Matavai.

In our passage to the ship, which we rowed in one hour, nothing but *Britannia* was inquired after, and of the number of ships and guns. When I told them we had ships of a hundred guns, they could not believe it, till I drew one on paper: they then asked me if it was not as big as Tarrah,

which is a high projecting headland, half way between Matavai and Oparre, called by us One-tree Hill. Tinah much wished that one of these large ships should be sent to Otaheite, and that myself should come in her, and bring him a number of things that he wanted; among which he particularly desired beds and high-backed elbow chairs might not be forgotten: a request perfectly according with the indolent character of Tinah.

Saturday, November 1st.—As we had occasion to fix a tent on Point Venus, this morning we moved the ship nearer to it, and moored again in six fathoms, the point bearing N.N.E.

Tinah and several other chiefs dined on board with me. After dinner I went on shore with Tinah, and made a visit to his father Otow. I likewise went to the garden which I had made near Poeeno's house, and found every thing had been taken care of. After this, I was invited to an entertainment called *Heiva*, which Tinah had ordered, and which consisted of singing and dancing by three men and a young girl. When this performance was finished I returned to the ship.

Sunday, 2nd.—At daylight I sent Mr. Christian with a party to erect our tent, and soon after followed myself with Tinah, Moannah, and Poeeno. With their consent I fixed a boundary, within which the natives were not to enter without leave, and the chiefs cautioned them against it.

The principal use of the tents on shore was for a lodgment for the plants; and I had now, instead of appearing to receive a favour, brought the chiefs to believe that I was doing them a kindness in carrying the plants as a present from them to the *Earee Rahie no Britanee*. The party at the tent consisted of nine persons, including Nelson and his assistant.

Tinah dined with me on board, and was to-day my only visitor: nevertheless, the ceremony of being fed he so scrupulously observed, that, even after all the attendants were sent away, and we were left by ourselves, I was obliged to lift the wine to his mouth. The wives of the *Earees* are sometimes subject to this restriction after the birth of a child, but are released after a certain time, on performing a ceremony called *Oamoa*.

After dinner, Tinah invited me to accompany him with a present of provisions to a party of the *Arreoys*, a society described in the accounts of the former voyages;* in this ceremony, he made me the principal person. Our way to the place where the offering was to be made, was by the side of a river, along the banks of which I had always walked before this time; but on the present occasion a canoe was provided for me, and dragged by eight men. On arriving at the landing-place, I saw a large quantity of bread-fruit, with some hogs ready dressed, and a quantity of cloth. At about forty yards distance sat a man, who, I was informed, was a principal *Arreoy*. A lane being made by the crowd, he was addressed by one of Tinah's people, standing on the canoe, in a speech composed of short sentences, which lasted about a quarter of an hour. During this, a piece of cloth was produced, one end of which I was desired to hold, and five men, one with a sucking pig, and the others having each a basket of bread-fruit,

* A licentious society admitting both men and women, between whom the intercourse is promiscuous; all children born in this society are immediately destroyed.

prepared to follow me. In this order we advanced to the *Arreoy*, and laid the whole down before him. I then spoke several sentences dictated to me by Tinah, the meaning of which I did not understand; and my pronunciation not being very exact, caused a great deal of mirth. This speech being finished, I was shown another *Arreoy*, who had come from Ulietea, and to him likewise I was required to deliver an oration. Tinah, understanding from me, that I had children in my own country, he desired me to make one more offering on their account. There still remained three baskets of bread-fruit, a small pig, and another piece of cloth: with these, assisted as before, I made the offering in favour of my children to the man whom I had first addressed. He made no reply to all my fine speeches, but sat with great gravity, and received every thing as a matter of right, and not of courtesy.

All that I could make out of this strange ceremony was, that the *Arreoys* are highly respected, and that the society is chiefly composed of men distinguished by their valour or some other merit, and that great trust and confidence is reposed in them; but I could not comprehend what this had to do with my children, or why it should be imagined that an offering made on their account to a society of men, who destroy all their children, should be propitious. I learnt from Tinah, in talking about his children, that his first-born child was killed as soon as it came into the world, he being then an *Arreoy*; but before his second child was born, he quitted the society. The *Arreoys* are allowed great latitude in their amours, except in times of danger. Then, as they are almost all fighting men (*taia toa*) they are restricted, that they may not weaken or enervate themselves.

These ceremonies being ended, I returned to the ship.

Such of the natives, as I conversed with about the institution of so extraordinary a society as the *Arreoy*, asserted that it was necessary, to prevent an over population. *Worrow worrow no to mydidde, worrow worrow te tata.* We have too many children, and too many men, was their constant excuse. Yet it does not appear, that they are apprehensive of too great an increase of the lower class of people, none of them being ever admitted into the *Arreoy* society. The most remarkable instance, related to me, of the barbarity of this institution, was of Teppahoo, the Earee of the district of Tettaha, and his wife, Tetteehowdeeah, who is sister to Otow, and considered as a person of the first consequence. I was told that they have had eight children, every one of which was destroyed as soon as born. That any human beings were ever so devoid of natural affection, as not to wish to preserve alive one of so many children, is not credible. It is more reasonable to conclude, that the death of these infants was not an act of choice in the parents; but that they were sacrificed in compliance with some barbarous superstition, with which we are unacquainted. What strengthens this conjecture is, that they have adopted a nephew as their heir, of whom they are excessively fond.

In countries so limited as the islands in the South Seas, the natives of which, before they were discovered by European navigators, probably had not an idea of the existence of other lands, it is not unnatural that an increasing population should occasion apprehensions of universal distress. Orders of celibacy, which have proved so prejudicial in other countries, might perhaps in this have been beneficial; so far at least as to have answered their purpose by means not criminal. The number of inhabitants at Otaheite have been estimated at above one hundred thousand. The island, however, is not cultivated to the greatest advantage: yet, were they continually to improve in husbandry, their improvement could not, for a length of time, keep pace with an unlimited population.

An idea here presents itself, which, however fanciful it may appear at first sight, seems to merit some attention:—While we see among these islands so great a waste of the human species, that numbers are born only to die; and, at the same time, a large continent so near them as New Holland, in which there is so great a waste of land uncultivated, and almost destitute of inhabitants; it naturally occurs, how greatly the two countries might be made to benefit each other; and gives occasion to regret that the islanders are not instructed in the means of emigrating to New Holland, which seems as if designed by nature to serve as an asylum for the superflux of inhabitants in the islands. Such a plan of emigration, if rendered practicable to them, might not only be the means of abolishing the horrid custom of destroying children, as it would remove the plea of necessity, but might lead to other important purposes. A great continent would be converted from a desert to a populous country; a number of our fellow-creatures would be saved; the inhabitants of the islands would become more civilized; and it is not improbable, but that our colonies in New Holland would derive so much benefit as to more than repay any trouble or expense, that might be incurred in endeavouring to promote so humane a plan.

The latter, however, is a remote consideration, for the intertropical parts of New Holland are those most suited to the habits and manner of living of the islanders; and likewise the soil and climate are the best adapted to their modes of agriculture. Man placed by his Creator in the warm climates, perhaps would never emigrate into the colder, unless under the tyrannous influence of necessity; and ages might elapse before the new inhabitants would spread to our settlers, though they are but barely within the limits of frost, that great cause of nine tenths of the necessities of Europeans. Nevertheless, besides forwarding the purposes of humanity and general convenience, in bringing a people without land to a land without people, the benefit of a mutual intercourse with a neighbouring and friendly colony, would in itself be no inconsiderable advantage.

Among people so free from ostentation as the Otaheiteans, and whose manners are so simple and natural, the strictness with which the punctilios of rank are observed, is surprising. I know not if any action, however meritorious, can elevate a man above the class in which he was born, unless he were to acquire sufficient power to confer dignity on himself. If any woman of the inferior classes has a child by an Earee, it is not suffered to live. Perhaps the offspring of Teppahoo and Tetteehowdeeah were destined to satisfy some cruel adjustment of rank and precedency.

CHAPTER VII.

A THEFT COMMITTED—DECEPTION OF THE PAINTED HEAD—
CONVERSATION WITH A PRIEST—A WRESTLING MATCH—
REPORTS OF THE NATIVES CONCERNING OTHER ISLANDS—
SOME ACCOUNT OF ORAI.

MONDAY, November 3rd.—The trade for provisions I directed to be carried on at the tent by Mr. Peckover, the gunner. Moannah likewise resided there, as a guard over his countrymen; but though it appeared to be the wish of all the chiefs, that we should remain unmolested, it was not possible entirely to prevent them from pilfering.

My table at dinner was generally crowded. Tinah, Oreepyah, Poeeno, and Moannah, were my regular guests, and I was seldom without some chiefs from other districts. Almost every individual of any consequence has several names, which makes it frequently perplexing, when the same person is spoken of, to know who is meant. Every chief has perhaps a dozen or more names in the course of thirty years; so that the person who has been spoken of by one visitor, will not perhaps be known to another, unless other circumstances lead to a discovery. The father of Tinah, at this time called Otow, was known in 1769 by the name of Whappai.

I showed Tinah the preparations I was making to take on board the bread-fruit plants, which pleased him exceedingly, but he did not forget to remind me, that when the next ship came out he hoped King George would send him large axes, files, saws, cloth of all kinds, hats, chairs, and bedsteads, with arms, ammunition, and in short every thing he could think of mentioning.

This afternoon, the gudgeon of the rudder belonging to the large cutter, was drawn out and stolen, without being perceived by the man that was stationed to take care of her. Several petty thefts having been committed by the natives, mostly owing to the negligence of our own people; and as these kind of accidents generally created alarm, and had a tendency to interrupt the good terms on which we were with the chiefs, I thought it would have a good effect to punish the boat-keeper in their presence, many of them happening to be then on board; and accordingly I ordered him a dozen lashes. Tinah, with several of the chiefs, attended the punishment, and interceded very earnestly to get it mitigated: the women showed great sympathy, and that degree of feeling which characterises the amiable part of their sex.

The natives brought off to-day two different kinds of roots that grow like yams; one they call Ettee, which is a sweet root, common also to the Friendly Islands, and may be eaten as a sweetmeat: the other they call Appay, a root like the Tyah or Eddie in the West Indies. A fruit called Ayyah, which is the jambo of Batavia, was likewise brought off to us: they are as large as middle-sized apples, very juicy and refreshing, and may be eaten in large quantities. Also some Avees, which are the real Otaheite apple; but they were not yet in season. These are a delicious high-flavoured fruit, and before they are ripe, answer the culinary purposes of our apples.

Tuesday, 4th.—A chief called Tootaha, who came from the island Ulietea, was introduced to me to-day, by Tinah, as one of his particular friends. I was told that he was a priest, and a person of great knowledge. I desired Tinah to take what he thought proper as a present for him; and I must do Tinah the justice to say, he was more sparing than I should have been. I likewise received a visit to-day from Oedidee, the man who had been at sea with Captain Cook in 1773 and 1774, as related in the account of that voyage. He still retained some of the English words which he had learnt in that expedition.

Wednesday, 5th.—The weather variable, with lightning, and frequent showers of rain. Wind E.N.E.

This was the first day of our beginning to take up plants: we had much pleasure in collecting them, for the natives offered their assistance, and perfectly understood the method of taking them up and pruning them.

The crowd of natives was not so great as hitherto it had been: the curiosity of strangers was satisfied; and, as the weather began to be unsettled and rainy, they had almost all returned to their homes; so that only the people of Matavai and Oparre remained with us, except a few chiefs from other islands: our supplies however were abundant; and what I considered as no small addition to our comforts, we ceased to be incommoded, when on shore, by the natives following us, and could take our walks almost unnoticed. In any house that we wished to enter, we always experienced a kind reception, and without officiousness. The Otaheiteans have the most perfect easiness of manners, equally free from forwardness and formality. When they offer refreshments, if they are not accepted, they do not think of offering them the second time; for they have not the least idea of that ceremonious kind of refusal which expects a second invitation. In like manner, at taking leave, we were never troubled with solicitations to prolong our visit, but went without ceremony, except making use of a farewell expression at parting. Another advantage, seldom found in warm countries, was, in this part of Otaheite, being free from muskitoes, though, at particular times of the year, the inhabitants are pestered with great numbers of flies.

Moannah continued our constant friend at the tent, and, with Tinah and all his friends, dined with me every day.

The ship's barber had brought with him from London, a painted head, such as the hair-dressers have in their shops, to show the different fashions of dressing hair; and it being made with regular features, and well coloured, I desired him to dress it, which he did with much neatness, and with a stick, and a quantity of cloth, he formed a body. It was then reported to the natives that we had an English woman on board, and the quarter-deck was cleared of the crowd, that she might make her appearance. Being handed up the ladder, and carried to the after-part of the deck, there was a general shout of "*Huaheine no Brittanne myty.*" Huaheine signifies woman, and myty, good. Many of them thought it was living, and asked if it was my wife. One old woman ran with presents of cloth and bread-fruit, and laid them at her feet; at last they found out the cheat; but continued all delighted with it, except the old lady, who felt herself mortified, and took back her presents, for which she was laughed at exceedingly. Tinah and all the chiefs enjoyed the joke, and, after making many inquiries about the British women, they strictly enjoined me, when I came again, to bring a ship full of them.

Some very fine sugar-cane was brought to me; each of the pieces was six inches round. I had before told Tinah that our sugar was made of it, and he was very desirous to discover the means; for they were so fond of our loaf sugar, that a present to any chief would have been incomplete without a piece of it. Another article in great estimation, and likewise expected to make part of a present, was scissors, which they made use of to keep their beards in order.

By this time Nelson had, with assistance from the ship, completed a large garden near the tents; in which were sown seeds of different kinds, that we had collected at the Cape of Good Hope. I likewise distributed fruit-stones and almonds for planting, among the chiefs, who, I hope, will endeavour to make them succeed: and, as they are very fond of sweet-smelling flowers, with which the women delight to ornament themselves, I gave them some rose-seed.

Thursday, 6th.—We had very variable weather, much rain, and some westerly winds; so that a considerable swell ran into the bay, and a number of spotted white and black porpoises made their appearance. I had the mortification to see that our garden-ground had been much trod over; and what was worse, the chiefs appeared but little concerned at it. To this kind of carelessness and indifference I attribute the miscarriage of many of the plants left here by Captain Cook. I had now in a flourishing state, two orange plants, some vines, a fig-tree, and two pine-apple plants, which I gave to Poeeno, whose residence is a place favourable for their growth.

We got on successfully with our plants, having a hundred potted at the tent, and in a fair way of doing well. The cabin also was completed, and ready to receive them on board.

I have before remarked that my friend Tinah was rather of a selfish disposition, and this afternoon he showed a stronger instance of it than I was witness to at any time before or after. His brother Oreepyah sent on board to me a present of a large hog and a quantity of bread-fruit; but these kind of presents are much more expensive than purchasing at the market. Soon after Oreepyah himself came on board. Tinah was with me at the time, and whispered me to tell Oreepyah not to bring any more hogs or fruit, and to take those back which he had sent. This advice, as may be supposed, did not produce the effect intended. Oreepyah appears to be a man of great spirit, and is highly respected by his countrymen. Among other visitors to-day was one of the men who had been to Lima in 1776.

Saturday, 8th.—Our plants had now increased to 252: as they were all kept on shore at the tent I augmented the guard there, though, from the general conduct of the natives, there did not appear the least occasion for so much caution.

While I was at dinner, Tinah desired I would permit a man to come down into the cabin, whom he called his Taowah, or priest; for I was obliged to keep a sentinel at the hatchway to prevent being incommoded at my meals with too much company; a restriction which pleased the chiefs, who always asked leave for any particular person

to be admitted of whom they wished me to take notice. The company of the priest brought on a religious conversation. He said their great God was called Oro; and that they had many others of less consequence. He asked me if I had a God?—if he had a son? and who was his wife? I told them he had a son, but no wife. Who was his father and mother? was the next question. I said he never had father or mother; at this they laughed exceedingly. You have a God then who never had a father or mother, and has a child without a wife? Many other questions were asked, which my little knowledge of the language did not enable me to answer.

The weather was now fine again, and a great number of people were come from other parts of the island. Tinah informed me that there was to be a heiva and a wrestling match on shore, and that the performers waited for our attendance; we therefore set off with several of our friends, and about a quarter of a mile from the tents we found a great concourse of people formed into a ring. As soon as we were seated, a dancing heiva began, which was performed by two girls and four men: this lasted half an hour, and consisted of wanton gestures and motions, such as have been described in the account of former voyages. When the dance ended, Tinah ordered a long piece of cloth to be brought; his wife Iddeah and myself were desired to hold the two first corners, and, the remaining part being supported by many others, we carried it to the performers and gave it them. Several other chiefs made a like present or payment. The performers were strollers, that travelled about the country as in Europe.

After this the wrestling began, and the place soon became a scene of riot and confusion. A party of the Arreoys also began to exercise a privilege, which it seems they are allowed, of taking from the women such of their clothes as they thought worth it; so that some of them were left little better than naked. One young woman, who was attacked, opposed them with all her strength, and held fast her cloth, though they almost dragged her along the ground. Observing that I took notice of her, she held out her hand, and begged my assistance; and at my request she escaped being pillaged.

Soon after a ring was again made, but the wrestlers were so numerous within it, that it was impossible to restore order. In the challenges, they lay one hand upon their breast, and on the bending of the arm at the elbow, with the other hand they strike a very smart blow, which, as the hand is kept hollow, creates a sound that may be heard at a considerable distance; and this they do so frequently, and with such force, that the flesh becomes exceedingly bruised, and, the skin breaking, bleeds considerably. At this time, the sound from so many resembled that of a number of people in a wood felling trees. This is the general challenge; but when any two combatants agree to a trial, they present their hands forward, joining them only by the extremities of the fingers. They begin by watching to take an advantage; at length they close, seize each other by the hair, and are most commonly parted before either receives a fall. Only one couple performed any thing like the part of good wrestlers; and, as they were an equal match, this conflict lasted longer than any of the others; but they also were parted.

Iddeah was the general umpire, and she managed with so much address as to prevent any quarrelling, and there was no murmuring at her decisions. As her person was large, she was very conspicuous in the circle. Tinah took no part in the management. Upon the whole, this performance gave me a better opinion of their strength than of their skill or dexterity.

For some time past Tinah had talked of going to the island of Tethuroa, which lies eight or ten leagues north from Otaheite, to fetch his mother; but I found I had only half understood him, for this morning he inquired when we were to sail there in the ship; however he seemed to feel no great disappointment at my not complying with his wish. Tethuroa, he informed me, is the property of his family. He likewise spoke to me about an island called Roo-opow, the situation of which he described to be to the eastward of Otaheite four or five days' sail, and that there were large animals upon it with eight legs. The truth of this account he very strenuously insisted upon, and wished me to go thither with him. I was at a loss to know whether or not Tinah himself gave credit to this whimsical and fabulous account; for though they have credulity sufficient to believe any thing, however improbable, they are at the same time so much addicted to that species of wit which we call humbug, that it is frequently difficult to discover whether they are in jest or earnest. Their ideas of geography are very simple; they believe the world to be a fixed plane of great extent, and that the sun, moon, and stars are all in motion round it. I have been frequently asked by them if I have not been as far as the sun and moon; for they think we are such great travellers that scarce any undertaking is beyond our ability.

Another island, called Tappuhoi, situated likewise to the eastward, was described to me by Tinah, the inhabitants of which were said to be all warriors, and that the people of Otaheite did not dare to go there. He told me, that very lately a canoe from Tappuhoi was at the island Maitea; that as soon as they landed they began to fight with the people of Maitea, who killed them all except a young lad and a woman, who have since been at Otaheite. I saw the boy, but could get no information from him. It is most probable, that this unfortunate visit of the canoe from Tappuhoi was not designed, but occasioned by adverse winds, which forced them so far from their own island; and that the people of Maitea began the attack, taking advantage of their superior numbers on account of some former quarrel.

Thursday, 13th.—I had a large company to dine with me to-day. Some of my constant visitors had observed that we always drank His Majesty's health as soon as the cloth was removed, but they were by this time become so fond of wine, that they would frequently remind me of the health in the middle of dinner, by calling out King George Earee no Brittannee, and would banter me if the glass was not filled to the brim. Nothing could exceed the mirth and jollity of these people when they met on board.

I was assured by Oediddee and several others, that the vines planted at the island Huaheine by Captain Cook had succeeded and bore fruit; and that some of the other plants, both at Huaheine and at Oaitepeha, a district on the S.E. part of Otaheite, had been preserved, and were in a thriving state. I was likewise informed that there was a bull and a cow alive at Otaheite, but on different parts of the island; the former at a place called Itteah, the latter at the district of Tettaha. All the rest were taken away or destroyed by the people of Eimeo. As Tettaha was at no great distance, I determined to go thither myself the first opportunity, and make inquiries, in hopes that the breed might still be preserved.

I had much discourse with my guests about Omai: they confirmed to me that he died about thirty months after Captain Cook left the islands. Soon after Captain Cook's departure from Huaheine, there were some disputes between the people of that island and those of Ulietea, in which also the natives of Bolabola took a part. Omai, who was become of consequence from the possessing three or four muskets and some ammunition, was consulted on the occasion. Such was his opinion and assurances of success, that a war was determined on, and took place immediately.— Victory soon followed, through the means of those few arms, and many of the Ulietea and Bolabola men were killed. In this contest their flints proved bad, or probably the locks of the muskets had got out of order: this they remedied by a lighted stick, one man presenting the musket, and another with the burnt stick setting fire to the priming; without which contrivance their arms would have proved useless. This expedition, it seems, consumed all their ammunition. Peace was soon after established, but I did not understand that Omai had increased his possessions or his rank. Nevertheless, I have reason to conclude, that he was in some degree of favour with his countrymen, from the general good character which they give of him. It appears that he always remembered England with kindness; for his accounts to his countrymen have been such as to give them, not only a great idea of our power and consequence, but of our friendship and goodwill towards him.

Tyvaroah, the eldest of the New Zealand boys that were left with him, died a short time after Omai. About Coah, the youngest, I had always doubtful accounts till I came to Huaheine, where I learnt that he likewise was dead.

CHAPTER VIII.

EXPEDITION TO TETTAHA AFTER A HEIFER—EXTRAORDINARY DOMESTIC ARRANGEMENTS—TINAH'S MOTHER VISITS THE SHIP—A SHEEP BROUGHT FROM ULIETEA—HEAVY STORM—DEATH OF THE SURGEON—TAOWNE AND TGARROAH HANDOURS EXAMINED.

AFTER dinner I went on shore, and while I was at the tents, from having exposed myself too much in the sun, I was taken ill, and continued in much pain for near an hour. This was soon known among the natives, and I was exceedingly surprised to see Tinah and all the principal people, both men and women, collecting round me and offering their assistance. For this short illness I was made ample amends, by the pleasure I received from the attention and appearance of affection in these kind people.

Friday, 14th November.—This morning I had numberless inquiries after my health. The weather being fine, I invited Tinah, Oreepyah, and Poceno, to accompany me to Tettaha, in order to inquire after the cow, and soon after sunrise we set off in the launch. Tettaha is nearly four leagues from Point Venus. On our arrival, Tinah sent a man to give notice of our visit. The chief of the district, whose name was Teppahoo, did not appear, but sent a messenger to demand, if I came only to see the cow, or to take it away with me? In answer to this, I sent assurances that I only desired to see it; and the chiefs who were with me spoke to the same effect. I was then desired to proceed in the boat further along shore to the westward. In our way Tinah made me stop among some fishing canoes to purchase fish for him, which he ate raw, with salt water for sauce. When we arrived at the landing-place, a great number of people had collected, and soon after Teppahoo arrived. Oreepyah and I went with him about a quarter of a mile, when I was shown one of the most beautiful heifers I ever saw. I asked if they had any more, but they all said there was no other than a bull at Itteah, as before-mentioned. I could not refrain from expressing my displeasure at the destruction and the foolish separation of these fine animals. I had shared with Captain Cook in the trouble of this business, and had been equally anxious for the success.

The district of Tettaha is not so luxuriant and fruitful as the country about Matavai. As I saw nothing of consequence to detain me, I made a present to Teppahoo, and, after inviting him to visit me on board the ship, which he promised to do, I took leave. Tinah had remained all this time in the boat. I observed that no respect was shown to him at this place, nor was he able to procure a cocoa-nut, or a bread-fruit, otherwise than by purchasing it. The heifer being here is a proof of this district not having been friendly to the people of Matavai and Oparre.

In our way back, having to row against the wind, we stopped to refresh at Oparre, and it was eight o'clock by the time we arrived at the ship. I kept my fellow-travellers on board to supper, and they did not fail to remind me of the king's health.

Monday, 17th.—Our collection of bread-fruit plants at the tents continued increasing. This morning I sent twelve on board, in pots, to discover where they would thrive the best, the air being more temperate on board the ship than on shore. While I was absent from the ship, Teppahoo had been on board, and left a hog as a present for me.

After dinner to-day, Tinah, who was my constant visitor, left the table sooner than usual. When he was gone, Oreepyah, his brother, and Oeddidee, told me a piece of scandal, which had been before hinted to me, but which till now I had not heard of with certainty: this was, that Iddeah, Tinah's wife, kept a gallant, who was a *towtow*, or servant, and the very person who always fed Tinah at dinner: and this was so far from being without Tinah's knowledge or consent, that they said it was by his desire. They added many other circumstances, and, as I appeared to doubt, they took several opportunities, in the course of the day, of mentioning it to other people, who all declared it was true.

Tuesday, 18th.—This afternoon, I saw Teppa-

hoo, and invited him on board: before we parted, I bargained with him for the heifer, which he promised to bring in five days. My intention was, that if I got the heifer, I would endeavour to purchase the bull at Itteah: but if that could not be done, then I could send the heifer as a present to the possessor of the bull, which might equally well answer my purpose.

It has been mentioned, that Tinah had a place in my cabin to keep those things which I gave him, as being more secure on board than on shore. I had remarked lately, that his hoard seemed to diminish the more I endeavoured to increase it: at length I discovered that Iddeah kept another hoard in the master's cabin, which she regularly enriched from her husband's, whenever I made him a present, apprehending that I should cease giving, when I saw Tinah's locker full. At his request, I set the carpenters to work to make him a chest large enough for himself and wife to sleep on. Captain Cook had formerly given him such a chest, but it had been taken from him by the Eimeo people.

Friday, 21st.—This forenoon, I received a message from Teppahoo, to acquaint me the heifer was brought to Matavai. I immediately went on shore, and found that he had been as good as his word. The purchase money was paid, which consisted of a shirt, a hatchet, a spike-nail, a knife, a pair of scissors, a gimlet, and file; to which was added, a small quantity of loaf-sugar. Teppahoo appeared well pleased with his bargain; and I sent the heifer to Poceno's residence, near which was plenty of grass.

In the afternoon, I was invited to a heiva, the most extraordinary part of which was an oration, with some ceremonies in compliment to us. Twelve men were divided into four ranks, with two women in the front; behind them all stood a priest, who made a speech which lasted ten minutes, and which was listened to with some attention. During this, the picture of Captain Cook, which had been brought for that purpose, was placed by my side. When the priest left off speaking, a piece of white cloth was wrapt round the picture, and another piece round me. The priest then spoke again for a short time, and an old man placed a piece of plaited cocoa-nut leaf at my feet; the same was done to Tinah, and one piece was put under the picture. After this the dancing began, which was in the same style that we had already seen.

The head of the ship was the figure of a woman, and not ill carved. As we were painting the ship's upper works, I directed this figure to be painted in colours, with which the islanders were much pleased. Not only the men, but the women, desired me to bring English women when I came again. To-day Oeddidee, thinking I was not convinced of the truth of what he had told me about Iddeah, mentioned the affair to the lady herself in my hearing, at which she laughed, but said he did ill to tell me of it. However, it was evident she was not much offended; for they were both very much diverted in discoursing upon the subject.

I find it is not at all uncommon for brothers to have connexion with the wives of each other, particularly elder brothers with the wives of their younger brothers, which is generally allowed, and no offence taken: but if any person, not belonging to the family, endeavours at the same intimacy, it is resented as an injury. Inclination seems to be the only binding law of marriage at Otaheite.

As I purposed to get instruments on shore at Point Venus, to make observations, I desired Tinah to order a house to be brought there for me; which was done, and fixed in half an hour, being only a light shed supported by posts.

Monday, 24th, I bought a turtle, that was caught on the reefs. As Tinah was going to leave me for a few days, I had it dressed for his dinner. He told me that his mother, Oberree-roah, was arrived from the island Tethuroa, and begged that I would send for her in the morning, and take care of her till he returned; which I willingly promised.

Tuesday, 25th.—This morning, I sent a boat to Oparre, which returned in the afternoon with Oberree-roah, and two women, her servants. As she was old and corpulent, it was with difficulty that we helped her up the ship's side. As soon as she was in the ship, she sat down on the gangway, and, clasping my knees in her arms, expressed her pleasure at seeing me by a flood of tears. Her servants then produced three pieces of cloth, which, with a large hog, some bread-fruit, plantains, and cocoa-nuts, she had brought as a present. As she was fatigued by her journey, she wished to remain on board all night; and I directed accommodations to be prepared, which was done with little trouble, as nothing more was necessary than a mat, and some cloth spread on the deck. She had with her a favourite cat, bred from one that had been given her by Captain Cook. She told me all the misfortunes that had befallen her son and friends, since Captain Cook left Otaheite. All the accounts agree in some of the cattle being now alive at the island Eimeo: in the number they differ; but that there are eight, is the least account. In the morning, Oberree-roah being desirous to go on shore, I made her a present of several things, which she did not care to take with her then, but requested that I would keep them safe for her. Only Moannah and Poeeno dined with me to-day. They told me that Tinah and his brother Oreepyah were not on good terms together; and it was imagined that they would fight as soon as the ship was gone. I had observed a coolness between them, and had at times endeavoured to make them more cordial, but with very little effect. Their quarrel has arisen from a disagreement between their wives.

In the afternoon, a canoe from Ulietea arrived, in which was an Earee, or chief, of that island, who is a nephew to Oberree-roah. He brought a sheep with him: the poor animal was infected with the mange, and in very poor condition. The climate had not, as far as I could judge, altered the quality of the wool, with which he was well covered, except a part about the shoulders. I imagine this animal to be the English ewe left by Captain Cook. The owner assured me that there were ten sheep at Huaheine; the truth of which I much doubted. I was surprized, and rather mortified, to find that he set so little value on this, as to let me have it, at the first word, for a small adze. I sent it to be kept at Poeeno's, with the heifer.

Friday, 28th.—Tinah and his wife returned to Matavai, and, from appearances which I have no reason to mistrust, were sincerely glad to see me again after their short absence. They brought, as usual, a present of a hog and fruit. This morning there was an eclipse of the sun, but the weather was so cloudy, that I had only an opportunity of observing the end of the eclipse, which was at 19^h 43' 53".

Saturday, 29th, I sent a man to shear the ewe, by which a remedy could more easily be applied to cure the disease with which it was infected. The garden made near the tents was not in a prosperous condition: most of the melons and cucumbers were destroyed by insects; and the soil, being sandy, was not favourable to the other seeds. I therefore chose another spot of ground, farther from the sea-side, and had an assortment of seeds sown.

Monday, December 1st.—In the night, the rudder of one of the boats was stolen from the tents. On landing in the morning, neither Tinah nor any of his family came near me, being, I was informed, afraid of my displeasure. As the loss was not great, I immediately sent to assure them that I had no anger, except against the person who committed the theft. In consequence of this message, Tinah and some of the other chiefs came to the tents, and promised that they would exert themselves to discover the thief, and get the rudder restored. This was the first theft, of any consequence, that had been committed since the tents were on shore; and my suspicions fell chiefly on the people who were here from some of the other islands. Tinah had just begun to build a house for himself, and I promised that our carpenters should assist him. Whydooah, the youngest brother of Tinah, had lately been one of my constant visitors, and seemed to have left off his former custom of getting drunk with the Ava. He was esteemed one of their best warriors; and I was told that in the quarrel with the people of Eimeo, he killed Maheine, the chief of that island.

Friday, 5th.—The weather for some time past had been very unsettled. This afternoon, the wind blew fresh from the N.W., which occasioned the sea to break very high across the Dolphin bank; and in the night such a heavy broken sea came into the bay, that we were obliged to batten all the hatchways down, and to keep everybody upon deck all night, though the rain came down in torrents. The ship rolled in a most violent manner. In the morning the wind increasing, and there being no possibility of putting to sea, we struck yards and topmasts, and trusted to our anchors. The river swelled so much with the rain, that the point of land on which the tents stood became an island; and, to preserve the bread-fruit plants from being endangered, the people were obliged to cut a passage for the river through a part of the beach, at a distance from the tents. The sea broke very high on the beach; nevertheless, a canoe put off, and, to my surprise, Tinah, his wife, and Moannah, made their way good through the surf, and came on board to see me. There was no other person in the canoe, for the weather did not admit of useless passengers: each of them had a paddle, which they managed with great activity and skill. These kind people embraced me with many tears, and expressed their apprehensions for the safety of the ship. Towards noon, however, the sea abated considerably, but the wind continued to blow strong from the N.W. At sun-set, Iddeah went on shore, but Tinah would remain with me the whole night.

Sunday, 7th.—The wind continued between the N. and N.W., but had so much moderated, that I no longer considered our situation to be alarming. At noon, Iddeah returned to the ship, with a large hog, and a supply of bread-fruit, and cocoa-nuts; and soon after, she and Tinah left the ship, having exacted a promise from me, that if the weather was moderate, I would go on shore in the morning, and visit their parents and sister, who, they told me, had been much alarmed on our account. I received a visit likewise from Poceno and his wife. This woman had always shown great regard for us; and now, on our meeting, before I could be aware of it, she began beating her head violently with a shark's tooth, so that her face was covered with blood in an instant. I put a stop to this as soon as I could, and, with the drying up of the blood, her agitation subsided. This ceremony is frequently performed, upon occasions either of joy or grief. Her husband said, that, if any accident happened to the ship, I should live with him, and that they would cut down trees, and build me another ship.

From this sample of the weather, and the information of the natives, I was convinced it would not be safe to continue in Matavai Bay much longer; and I determined to get every thing ready for sailing as speedily as I could.

The night proved moderate; and in the morning, I went on shore, where I was received by Oberree-roah, and several other friends, with great affection.

The plants received no injury from the bad weather, having been carefully covered from the spray of the sea: some were in a dormant state, and others were striking out young shoots. Nelson thought that it was better to refrain a few days from taking them on board; I therefore consented to defer it. He was of opinion that the plants could be propagated from the roots only, and I directed some boxes to be filled, as we could stow them where no others could be placed.

Tuesday, 9th.—This afternoon, in hauling the launch on shore to be repaired, many of the natives assisting, one of them, a fine boy about ten years old, was thrown down, and a roller which was placed under the boat went over him. The surgeon being ill, I sent off for his assistant. Fortunately no limb was broken, nor did he receive any material injury. The surgeon had been a long time ill, the effect of intemperance and indolence. He had latterly scarce ever stirred out of his cabin, but was not apprehended to be in a dangerous state; nevertheless, this evening he appeared to be so much worse than usual, that it was thought necessary to remove him to some place where he could have more air; but to no effect, for he died in an hour afterwards. This unfortunate man drank very hard, and was so averse to exercise, that he never would be prevailed on to take half a dozen turns upon deck at a time, in the whole course of the voyage.

Wednesday, 10th.—As I wished to bury the surgeon on shore, I mentioned it to Tinah; who said there would be no objection, but that it would be necessary to ask his father's consent first; which he undertook to do, and immediately left

me for that purpose. By this circumstance it appears, that though the eldest son of an Earee succeeds to the title and honours of the father as soon as he is born, yet a considerable portion of authority remains with the father, even after the son is of age. When Tinah returned, I went with him to the spot intended for the burial place, taking with us two men to dig the grave; but on our arrival, I found the natives had already begun it. Tinah asked me, if they were doing right? "There," says he, "the sun rises, and there it sets." The idea that the grave should be east and west, I imagine they learnt from the Spaniards, as the captain of one of their ships was buried at Oeitepeha in 1774. Certain it is, they had not the information from any body belonging to our ship; for I believe we should not have thought of it. The grave, however, was marked out very exactly. At four in the afternoon, the body was interred: the chiefs, and many of the natives, came to see the ceremony, and showed great attention during the service. Some of the chiefs were very inquisitive about what was to be done with the surgeon's cabin, on account of apparitions. They said, when a man died in Otaheite, and was carried to the Tupapow, that as soon as night came, he was surrounded by spirits, and if any person went there by himself, they would devour him: therefore they said that not less than two people together should go into the surgeon's cabin for some time. I did not endeavour to dissuade them from this belief, otherwise than by laughing, and letting them know that we had no such apprehensions.

In the afternoon, the effects of the deceased were disposed of, and I appointed Mr. Thomas Denham Ledward, the surgeon's mate, to do duty as surgeon.

Sunday, 14th.—This forenoon, we performed divine service. Many of the principal natives attended, and behaved with great decency. Some of the women at one time betrayed an inclination to laugh at our general responses; but, on my looking at them, they appeared much ashamed. After the service, I was asked if no offering was to be made for the Eatua to eat.

The weather had been fair all the last week, and at this time appeared quite settled; so that I was under no apprehensions of danger from continuing a little longer in Matavai bay.

———

CHAPTER IX.

A WALK INTO THE COUNTRY—THE OREAH ROAH—PREVAILED ON, BY THE KINDNESS OF THE CHIEFS, TO DEFER OUR DEPARTURE—BREAD-FRUIT PLANTS COLLECTED—MOVE THE SHIP TO TOARROAH HARBOUR—FISHING—THREE OF THE SHIP'S COMPANY DESERT—INDISCRETION OF OUR PEOPLE ON SHORE—INSTANCES OF JEALOUSY—MOURNING—BULL BROUGHT TO OPARRE BY A PROPHET—THE DESERTERS RECOVERED—TINAH PROPOSES TO VISIT ENGLAND.

WEDNESDAY, 17th Dec.—This morning I took a walk into the country, accompanied by Nelson and my old friend Moannah. The breadth of the border of low land, before we arrived at the foot of the hills, was near three miles. This part of our journey was through a delightful country, well covered with bread-fruit and cocoa-nut trees, and strewed with houses, in which were swarms of children. We then proceeded along a valley, still among houses, with plantations of yams, tarro, the cloth-plant, and their favourite root the Ava: there were bread-fruit trees on the sides of the hills, which were dwarfs in comparison of those on the low land. Our walk was very much interrupted by a river, the course of which was so serpentine, that we had to cross it several times, being carried over on men's shoulders.

On arriving at a Morai, I saw a number of the natives collected, and was informed that the priests were performing their devotions. Sixteen men were sitting on their heels; in the front was a pole covered with a plaited cocoa-nut branch, and before each of the men there was a number of small pieces of the same leaf plaited, which they call *hahyree*, and each had likewise a piece round his wrist. One, who appeared to be the chief priest, prayed aloud, and was answered by all the rest together: after a few short sentences and responses, they rose, and each carried an hahyree, which they placed at the foot of the pole, and returned to prayer: this was repeated till all the hahyree were delivered, and then the ceremony ended. I must not forget to mention, that they had placed, near the pole, an offering of plantains and bread-fruit, which they left for the Eatua. They very kindly asked us to partake of a roasted hog, that had been prepared for them whilst they were praying; but as I wished to make the most of the morning, before the sun was too high, I declined their offer, and Moannah bespoke refreshments to be ready for us when we returned.

We continued our walk up the valley, which became very narrow, and had advanced a considerable way beyond all the houses and plantations, when we were suddenly stopped by the cascade, that fell into the river from a height of above 200 feet: the fall at this time was not great, but in the heavy rains must be considerable. The natives look upon this as the most wonderful sight in the island. The fall of water is the least curious part; the cliff, over which it comes, is perpendicular, forming an appearance as if supported by square pillars of stone, and with a regularity that is surprising. Underneath is a pool eight or nine feet deep, into which the water falls; and in this place all the natives make a point of bathing once in their lives, probably from some religious idea.

The hills here approach each other within a few yards, and are well covered with wood. As the road appeared difficult, I did not care to proceed towards the mountain. I cannot with certainty say how far this curious precipice is from the bay, but think, in the road by which we went, it cannot be less than seven miles. It is called Peeah Roah.

In our return, we found a young pig prepared for us, and we made a hearty meal. We dined in the house of an old acquaintance of Nelson's; for whom he had, in 1777, planted the two shaddock plants, formerly mentioned, which he had brought from the Friendly Islands. These we had the satisfaction to see were grown to fine trees, and full of fruit.

In their plantations they do not take much pains, except with the Ava and the cloth-plant, both of which they are careful to keep clear of weeds. Many of the plantations of the cloth-plant were fenced with stone, and surrounded with a ditch.

The yams and plantains are mostly on the higher grounds. As soon as we had finished our dinner, we returned towards the ship. I was much delighted, in this walk, with the number of children that I saw in every part of the country: they are very handsome and sprightly, and full of antic tricks. They have many diversions that are common with the boys in England; such as flying kites, cat's cradle, swinging, dancing or jumping in a rope, walking upon stilts, and wrestling.

Friday, 19th.—The wind to-day blew fresh, but continued regular from the E. and E.S.E. We had likewise much rain, and a long swell set into the bay. I had not yet determined, whether, on leaving Matavai bay, I would go to the island Eimeo, or to the harbour of Toahroah near Oparre: this uncertainty made Tinah, and the rest of my friends, very anxious; and they appeared much distressed on my desiring them, this afternoon, to send on board all the things which they wished to have repaired by the forge, without delay, that what they wanted might be done before the ship left Matavai, which I told them would be in a few days. They very earnestly intreated I would stay one month longer. I represented this as impossible, and asked Tinah if he would not go with me to Eimeo; but he said, that, notwithstanding my protection, he was certain the Eimeo people would watch for an opportunity to kill him. He remained on board with me all night, but his wife went on shore, and returned early in the morning, bringing with her some axes, and other things, that were in need of repair.

When I went on shore, I found Otow, Oberreeroah, Moannah, and several others, in great tribulation at the thoughts that we were so soon to leave them. All the people of Matavai, I saw, were much concerned at my intention of going to Eimeo, and took every opportunity to prejudice me against the people of that island; to which I paid very little attention, as their motive was obvious. Their expressions of friendship and affection for me, however, I could not disregard, as I had no doubt of their being genuine and unaffected; and I felt my unwillingness to leave these kind people so much increased, that the next day, I sent the master in the launch to re-examine the depth of water between this bay and Toahroah harbour. He returned in the evening, and acquainted me, that he found a good bottom, with not less than sixteen fathoms depth all the way. The harbour of Toahroah appearing every way safe, I determined to get the ship there as speedily as possible, and I immediately made my intention public, which occasioned great rejoicing.

Wednesday, 24th.—This day, we took the plants on board, being 774 pots, all in a healthy state; for whenever any plant had an unfavourable appearance, it was replaced by another. The number of those rejected was, 302, of which not one in ten but was found to be growing at the root.

The natives reckon eight kinds of the bread-fruit tree, each of which they distinguish by a different name. 1. *Patteah*. 2. *Eroroo*. 3. *Awanna*. 4. *Mi-re*. 5. *Oree*. 6. *Powerro*. 7. *Appeere*. 8. *Rowdeeah*. In the first, fourth, and eighth class, the leaf differs from the rest; the fourth is more sinuated; the eighth has a large broad leaf, not at all sinuated. The difference of the fruit is principally in the first and eighth class. In the first, the fruit is rather larger and more of an oblong form: in the eighth, it is round and not above half the size of the others. I inquired if plants could be produced from the seed, and was told they could not, but that they must be taken from the root. The plants are best collected after wet weather, at which time the earth balls round the roots, and they are not liable to suffer by being moved.

The most common method of dividing time at Otaheite is by moons; but they likewise make a division of the year into six parts, each of which is distinguished by the name of the kind of bread-fruit then in season. In this division they keep a small interval called *Tawa*, in which they do not use the bread-fruit. This is about the end of February, when the fruit is not in perfection; but there is no part of the year in which the trees are entirely bare.

Thursday, 25th.—At day-light we unmoored, and I sent the tents in the launch to Oparre, with directions that after landing them, the launch should meet the ship in the entrance of Toahroah harbour, to show the safest part of the channel. At half past ten, we got the ship under sail, and run down under top-sails: when we were near the launch, it fell calm, and the ship shot past her. We immediately let the anchor go, but, to our great surprise, we found the ship was aground forwards. She had run on so easy, that we had not perceived it at the time. This accident occasioned us much trouble, as we were obliged to send anchors out astern to get the ship afloat: in doing this, one of the cables swept a rock, and was not got clear again without much difficulty. When the ship was moored, point Venus bore N. 46° E. The east point of the harbour N. 65° E. ¼ of a mile. Our distance from the shore half a cable's length; depth of water 8½ fathoms.

The next morning, on my landing, I was welcomed by all the principal people; I may say by the whole crowd, and congratulated on the safety of the ship. Tinah showed me a house near the water side, abreast the ship, which he desired I would make use of, and which was large enough for all our purposes. He and his brother Oree-pyah then desired I would stay and receive a formal address and present, which they called Otee. To this I assented, and a stool was brought for me to sit on. They then left me with Moan-nah, and in a short time I saw Tinah returning with about twenty men, who all made a stop at some distance, and a priest said a short prayer to the Eatua, to which the rest made reply. A man was then sent to me three several times, at each time bringing me a small pig, and the stem of a plantain leaf. The first they told me was for the God of Brittannee, the next for King George, and the last for myself. Moannah then got up, and, without being dictated to, made an oration for me; the purport of which I understood to be, that I received their offering with thanks; that we were good people and friends; and therefore he exhorted them to commit no thefts: he told them to bring their pigs, cocoa-nuts, and bread-fruit, and they would receive good things in return; that we took nothing without their consent; and finally, that every man was to quit the place (the house we occupied) at night; for if they made

any visit in the dark, they would be killed. With this speech the ceremony ended.

I found this a delightful situation, and in every respect convenient. The ship was perfectly sheltered by the reefs in smooth water, and close to a fine beach without the least surf. A small river, with very good water, runs into the sea about the middle of the harbour. I gave directions for the plants to be landed, and the same party to be with them as at Matavai. Tinah fixed his dwelling close to our station.

Monday, 29th.—Some of the natives took advantage of the butcher's negligence, and stole his cleaver. I complained of this to the chiefs who were on board, and they promised that they would endeavour to recover it; but an article so valuable as this was to the natives, I had no great expectation of seeing restored.

The ship continued to be supplied by the natives as usual. Cocoa-nuts were in such plenty, that I believe not a pint of water was drunk on board the ship in the twenty-four hours. Bread-fruit began to be scarce, though we purchased, without difficulty, a sufficient quantity for our consumption: there was, however, another harvest approaching, which they expected would be fit for use in five or six weeks. The better kind of plantains also were become scarce; but a kind which they call Vayhee were in great plenty. This fruit does not hang on the trees like the other kinds, but grows upon an upright stalk of considerable strength and substance. Though this plantain is inferior in quality to most of the others, it affords great subsistence to the natives. We received, almost every day, presents of fish, chiefly dolphin and albacore, and a few small rock fish. Their fishing is mostly in the night, when they make strong lights on the reefs, which attract the fish to them. Sometimes, in fine weather, the canoes are out in such numbers, that the whole sea appears illuminated. In the canoes they fish with hook and line, and on the reefs they strike the fish with a spear. Some likewise carry out small nets, which are managed by two men. In the day-time their fishing canoes go without the reefs, sometimes to a considerable distance, where they fish with rods and lines, and catch bonetas, and other fish. Whenever there is a show of fish, a fleet of canoes immediately proceeds to sea. Their hooks being bright, are used without bait, in the manner of our artificial flies. Their rods are made of bamboo; but when there are any very large fish, they make use of an out-rigger over the fore part of the canoe, about twenty-five feet in length, which has two prongs at the extremity, to each of which is fastened a hook and line; and when a fish takes the hook, it is raised by ropes managed by two men in the stern of the canoe.

1789. January 1st.—Contrary to my expectation, Tinah, this afternoon, brought on board the cleaver that had been stolen. The thief had taken it to Attahooroo, and Tinah told me, which I could not believe, that it was given up with great reluctance. The next morning I offered Tinah a present of axes, and other things; but, as he suspected it was meant by way of return for getting the cleaver restored, he would not be prevailed on to accept a single article.

I had constantly the company of Tinah himself, and some of his relations; but the royal children though so near us, never came in sight of the ship. The river separated them from the place occupied by our people on shore; and, for fear of giving alarm or offence, I gave strict orders that no one should attempt to go near their place of residence.

Monday, 5th.—At the relief of the watch, at four o'clock this morning, the small cutter was missing. I was immediately informed of it, and mustered the ship's company; when it appeared, that three men were absent, Charles Churchill, the ship's corporal, and two of the seamen, William Musprat, and John Millward; the latter of whom had been sentinel from twelve to two in the morning. They had taken with them eight stand of arms and ammunition; but what their plan was, or which way they had gone, no one on board seemed to have the least knowledge. I went on shore to the chiefs, and soon received information, that the boat was at Matavai; and that the deserters had departed in a sailing canoe for the island Tethuroa. On this intelligence, I sent the master to Matavai to search for the small cutter, and one of the chiefs went with him; but before they had got half way, they met the boat with five of the natives, who were bringing her back to the ship. This service, rendered me by the people of Matavai, pleased me much, and I rewarded the men accordingly.

I told Tinah, and the other chiefs, that I expected they would get the deserters brought back; for that I was determined not to leave Otaheite without them. They assured me, that they would do every thing in their power to have them taken; and it was agreed, that Oreepyah and Moannah should depart the next morning for Tethuroa. Oreepyah inquired if they had pocket pistols, "for," said he, "though we may surprize and seize them before they can make use of their muskets; yet, if they have pistols, they may do mischief, even while they are held." I quieted these apprehensions, by assuring them that the deserters had no pistols with them.

At day-light, Oreepyah and Moannah set off in two canoes for Tethuroa, but the weather became so boisterous, that they were obliged to return in the forenoon, and I was happy to see them get safe in, as the sea ran very high without the harbour. From the first of this month, the weather and winds had been much unsettled, with a great deal of rain. Our former station at Matavai appeared not at all safe, the sea at times breaking high over the Dolphin bank, and making a great swell in the bay. Oreepyah and Moannah both promised me, that they would sail again as soon as the weather should be fine.

Friday, 9th.—The wind continued to blow strong at sea, though in the harbour we had, at times, but light breezes. Poeeno from Matavai, came to see me to-day: he said, he was apprehensive that I was displeased with him, on account of our deserters having been carried to Tethuroa, by a canoe from Matavai. This, he declared, had been done before he heard of it; and that the only service in his power, he had not neglected to do for me, which was the sending our boat back. As this was really an act of friendship, I received him with great cordiality; and he assured me, that there could be no doubt, from the directions Tinah had given, of the deserters being brought to the ship, as soon as the weather would admit canoes to go after them.

Saturday, 10th.—One of the officers, this morning, on shore, inadvertently plucked a branch from a tree called Tutuee, that bears the oil nut, which was growing at a Morai. On entering with it into the house occupied by our people, all the natives, both men and women, immediately went away. When I went on shore, I found this branch tied to one of the posts of the house, although the effect it had on the natives was known. I was much displeased at this piece of wantonness, and ordered the branch to be taken away; but the natives, notwithstanding, would not come near the place. They said the house was *taboo*, which I understand to signify interdicted, and that none of them might approach it till the *taboo* was taken off, which could only be done by Tinah. To take any thing away from a Morai is regarded as a kind of sacrilege, and, they believe, gives great offence to the Eatua. At my request, Tinah took off the *taboo*, but not before the afternoon. This was performed by an offering of a plantain leaf at the Morai, and a prayer made to the Eatua. After this ceremony, the house was resorted to by the natives, as usual.

I had not yet given up the hope of obtaining the bull from Itteah, though I had hitherto received no satisfactory answer to the messages which Tinah had sent at my desire: I therefore spoke to Poeeno, who undertook to negotiate this business, and I commissioned him to make very liberal offers. He left me after dinner, to return to Matavai. In the evening, a messenger arrived from him, to acquaint me, that, in his absence, the sheep which I had trusted to his care, had been killed by a dog; and that he had sent the culprit, hoping that I would kill him for the offence he had committed. This poor sheep had been so much diseased, that I could not help suspecting he died without the dog's assistance, and that the story of the dog was invented to prevent my attributing it to want of care. This doubt did not appear in my answer; as for the dog, I told the messenger to do with him what he pleased.

Tuesday, 13th.—This morning, the weather being more moderate than it had been for some days past, Oreepyah sailed with two canoes for Tethuroa. Some business prevented Moannah from accompanying him, but he followed the next day with two other canoes. The wood that we had got at Matavai being expended, I applied to Tinah, who sent three trees down to the water side before night, which when cut up made a good launch load.

I saw two instances of jealousy to-day, one of which had nearly produced fatal consequences. A man was detected with a married woman, by the husband, who stabbed him in the belly with a knife: fortunately the intestines escaped, and the wound did not prove dangerous. The other instance was, a girl, who had constantly lived with my coxswain, beating another girl, that she discovered to have been too intimate with him.

Friday, 16th.—In walking to-day with Tinah near a Tupapow, I was surprised by a sudden outcry of grief. As I expressed a desire to see the distressed person, Tinah took me to the place, where we found a number of women, one of whom was the mother of a young female child that lay dead. On seeing us their mourning not only immediately ceased, but to my astonishment, they all burst into an immoderate fit of laughter, and, while we re-rained, appeared much diverted with our visit. I told Tinah the woman had no sorrow for her child, otherwise her grief would not have so easily subsided; on which he jocosely told her to cry again: they did not, however, resume their mourning in our presence. This strange behaviour would incline us to think them hard-hearted and unfeeling, did we not know that they are fond parents, and, in general, very affectionate: it is therefore to be ascribed to their extreme levity of disposition; and it is probable, that death does not appear to them with so many terrors, as it does to people of a more serious cast.

Sunday, 18th.—I received a message from Poeeno, to acquaint me that he had been successful in his negotiation for the bull, which he had driven part of the way by land, but could not get farther on account of the rivers, and therefore desired a boat should be sent for him. I accordingly ordered the launch to be got ready, and at two o'clock the next morning, Mr. Fryer, the master, set off in her.

In the afternoon, the launch returned with the bull, and my friend Poeeno. For the night I directed that the bull should remain at Oparre, and the next day he was taken to the cow at Matavai.

Wednesday, 21st.—To-day, Poeeno brought to me the person from whom he had the bull, to receive the stipulated payment, which was one of every article of traffic that I had in my possession. This man, whose name was Oweevee, they told me, was inspired by a divine spirit; and that in all matters of consequence he was consulted, for that he conversed with the Eatua. It was, they said, the Eatua that ordered him to demand the bull from Tinah, which not to have complied with, would have been the height of impiety. I endeavoured to convince them of the roguery of this man, thinking I had a fair argument to prove it by his selling that which the Eatua had ordered him to keep; but here I was easily defeated, for it seems the Eatua told him to sell me the beast. This being the case, I said I would not give the animals to any person; that they were now mine, and that I would leave them under the protection of Poeeno and Tinah, who I hoped would take care of them for me till I returned. They both entered into my views, and promised the animals should be attended to, and told me, that while they were considered as my property, no one would attempt to take them away.

Thursday, 22nd.—This afternoon, I received a message from Teppahoo, to inform me that our deserters had passed this harbour, and were at Tettaha, about five miles distant. I ordered the cutter to be got ready, and a little before sun-set left the ship, taking Oedidee with me. By his advice I landed at some distance from the place where the deserters were; but thinking it necessary to have the boat within call, and Oedidee assuring me that there was safe landing farther on, I directed the boat to proceed along shore, whilst Oedidee and I walked along the beach. The night was very dark and windy, and the shore being rocky, I soon lost sight of the boat. A few of the natives had joined us in our walk; and, from their manner, I had reason to suspect them of a design to close upon us, with an intention, no doubt, to plunder: I was provided with pocket-pistols, and

on producing one, they left us. Oedidee was so much alarmed that I could scarcely prevail on him to proceed. When we arrived at Teppahoo's house, we were very kindly received by him and his wife. The cutter was arrived, but, there being a very high surf, she could not come within a hundred yards of the shore.

The deserters, I was informed, were in a house close to us, and I imagined there would be no great difficulty in securing them, with the assistance of the natives. They had, however, heard of my arrival; and when I was near the house, they came out, without their arms, and delivered themselves up. I sent directions off to the boat for one of my people to come on shore, and for the boat to return to the place where I landed. My next business was to secure the arms, which I delivered to Teppahoo to take charge of for the night. One musket and two bayonets were missing, which they said were lost, by the canoe in which they came from Tethuroa having overset. I then took leave of Teppahoo, who presented us with a plentiful supply of provisions, and we proceeded with the deserters towards the boat; but as the wind had increased, and it rained hard, I determined to remain on shore till the morning; and having found shelter for the people, we passed the remainder of the night without accident. At daylight, I sent for the arms, and we returned to the ship.

I learnt from the deserters, that at Tethuroa they had seen Oreepyah and Moannah, who had made an attempt to secure them. They said it was their intention to have returned to the ship; and it is probable that they were so much harassed by the natives watching for an opportunity to surprise them, that they might wish to have the merit of returning of their own accord, to avoid the disgrace of being seized and brought back. At the time they delivered themselves up to me, it was not in their power to have made resistance, their ammunition having been spoiled by the wet.

In consequence of my having been kept all night from the ship by the tempestuous weather, the time-keeper went down at 10h. 5m. 36s. Its rate, previous to this, was 1s, 7 losing in 24 hours, and its error from the mean time at Greenwich was 7′ 29″, 2 too slow. I set it going again by a common watch, corrected by observations, and endeavoured to make the error the same as if it had not stopped; but being over cautious, made me tedious in setting it in motion, and increased the error from mean time at Greenwich. The rate of going I did not find to have altered.

At dinner Tinah congratulated me on having recovered my men, but expressed some concern that they had not been brought by Oreepyah and Moannah; lest I should imagine they had not done every thing in their power. To this I replied, that I was perfectly satisfied of their good intentions to serve me, and that I considered myself under great obligations to them for the trouble they had been at on my account. I learnt afterwards that they had actually seized and bound the deserters, but had been prevailed upon, by fair promises of their returning peaceably to the ship to let them loose: the deserters, however, finding an opportunity to get possession of their arms again, set the natives at defiance.

Friday, 30th.—This afternoon I punished

of the seamen, Isaac Martin, with nineteen lashes, for striking an Indian. This was a transgression of so serious a nature, and such a direct violation of my orders, that I would on no account be prevailed on to forgive it, though great intercession was made by some of the chiefs.

Oreepyah and Moannah were not yet returned from Tethuroa. This place is resorted to by the principal people of this part of Otaheite, at particular seasons, when fish are in great plenty there. It was described to me to be a group of small keys, surrounded by a reef: their produce is chiefly cocoa-nuts and plantains. During the season, bread-fruit and other provisions are daily carried over from Otaheite. Not less than a hundred sail of canoes were at Tethuroa when our deserters were there.

Teppahoo and his wife were become my constant visitors : he had for some time past been ill, and had made Oparre his place of residence, for the benefit of our surgeon's advice and assistance. At this time he complained of a hoarseness and sore-throat. Mr. Ledward, on examining him, discovered there had been two holes in the roof of his mouth, which, though healed, had the appearance of having been large : the adjacent parts appeared sound, yet the surgeon was of opinion that they were cancerous, and would in the end occasion his death.

Saturday, 31st.—This morning I ordered all the chests to be taken on shore, and the inside of the ship to be washed with boiling water to kill the cockroaches. We were constantly obliged to be at great pains to keep the ship clear of vermin, on account of the plants.—By the help of traps and good cats, we were freed from rats and mice. When I was at Otaheite with Captain Cook, there were great numbers of rats about all the houses, and so tame, that they flocked round the people at their meals for the offals, which were commonly thrown to them ; but, at this time, we scarce ever saw a rat, which must be attributed to the industry of a breed of cats left here by European ships.

After breakfast, I walked with Tinah to Matavai, to see the cattle and the gardens. Tinah had already taken so large a dose of the Ava, that he was perfectly stupified. Iddeah, however, was with us, and she is one of the most intelligent persons I met with at Otaheite.

We went first to Poeeno's house, and saw the bull and cow together in a very fine pasture. I was informed that the cow had taken the bull ; so that, if no untoward accident happens, there is a fair chance of the breed being established. In the garden, near Poeeno's house, many things had failed. The Indian corn was in a fine state, and I have no doubt but they will cultivate it all over the country. A fig-tree was in a very thriving way, as were two vines, a pine-apple plant, and some slips of a shaddock-tree. From this place we walked to the garden at Point Venus; but I had the mortification to find almost every thing there destroyed by the hogs. Some underground peas and Indian corn had escaped, and likewise the calitoo green and corn of Jamaica.

We returned to the ship ; and after dinner I was not a little surprised to hear Tinah seriously propose that he and his wife should go with me to England. He said he would only take two servants ; that he much wished to see King George, who, he was sure, would be glad to see him. Tinah and many of his countrymen were become extremely eager to get a knowledge of other countries, and were continually inquiring about the situations of the islands which we told them of in these seas. To quiet his importunity, I was obliged to promise that I would ask the king's permission to carry them to England, if I came again ; that then I should be in a larger ship, and could have accommodations properly fitted up. I was sorry to find, that Tinah was apprehensive he should be attacked by his enemies, as soon as our ship left Otaheite, and that if they joined, they would be too powerful for him. The illness of Teppahoo, with whom he was on good terms, gave him much uneasiness ; Teppahoo's wife being a sister of Otow's and aunt to Tinah. They have no children, as has been before related ; and if Teppahoo were to die, he would be succeeded, as Earee of the district of Tettaha, by his brother, who is an enemy to Tinah. I have on every occasion endeavoured to make the principal people believe that we should return again to Otaheite, and that we should revenge any injury done in our absence to the people of Matavai and Oparre.

The wife of Oedidee is likewise an aunt to Tinah, and sister to Otow. His native place is Ulietea, where he has some property ; but which, I imagine, is not of such consequence to him as the countenance of the chiefs with whom he is connected at Otaheite.

CHAPTER X.

THE SHIP'S CABLE CUT IN THE NIGHT—COOLNESS WITH THE CHIEFS ON THAT ACCOUNT—VISIT TO AN OLD LADY—DISTURBANCE AT A HEIVA—TINAH'S HOSPITALITY—A THIEF TAKEN, AND PUNISHED—PREPARATIONS FOR SAILING.

TUESDAY, February 3d.—I was present, this afternoon, at a wrestling match, where a young man, by an unlucky fall, put his arm out of joint at the elbow : three stout men immediately took hold of him, and two of them fixing their feet against his ribs, replaced it. I had sent for our surgeon, but before he arrived, all was well, except a small swelling of the muscles in consequence of the strain. I inquired what they would have done if the bone had been broken ; and, to shew me their practice, they got a number of sticks and placed round a man's arm, which they bound with cord. That they have considerable skill in surgery is not to be doubted. I have before mentioned an instance of an amputated arm being perfectly healed, and which had every appearance of having been treated with great propriety.

The part of the beach nearest the ship, was become the general place of resort towards the close of the day. An hour before sunset, the inhabitants began to collect, and here they amused themselves with exercising the lance, dancing, and various kinds of merriment, till nearly dark, when they retired to their homes. Of this cheerful scene, we were spectators and partakers, every fine evening.

Friday, 6th.—An occurrence happened to-day that gave me great concern, not only on account of the danger with which the ship had been threatened, but as it tended greatly to diminish the confidence and good understanding which had hitherto been constantly preserved between us and the natives. The wind had blown fresh in the night, and at day-light we discovered that the cable, by which the ship rode, had been cut near the water's edge in such a manner, that only one strand remained whole. While we were securing the ship, Tinah came on board. I could not but believe he was perfectly innocent of the transaction; nevertheless, I spoke to him in a very peremptory manner, and insisted upon his discovering and bringing to me the offender. I was wholly at a loss how to account for this malicious act. My suspicions fell chiefly, I may say wholly, on the strangers that came to us from other parts of the island; for we had, on every occasion, received such unreserved and unaffected marks of good-will from the people of Matavai and Oparre, that in my own mind I entirely acquitted them. The anger which I expressed, however, created so much alarm, that old Otow and his wife (the father and mother of Tinah) immediately quitted Oparre, and retired to the mountains in the midst of heavy rain, as did Teppahoo and his family. Tinah and Iddeah remained, and expostulated with me on the unreasonableness of my anger against them. He said that he would exert his utmost endeavours to discover the guilty person; but it might possibly not be in his power to get him delivered up, which would be the case, if he was either of Tiarraboo, Attahooroo, or of the island Eimeo. That the attempt might have been made as much out of enmity to the people of Matavai and Oparre as to me; every one knowing the regard I had for them, and that I had declared I would protect them against their enemies. All this I was inclined to believe; but I did not think proper to appear perfectly satisfied, lest Tinah, who was naturally very indolent, should be remiss in his endeavours to detect the offender. To guard as much as possible against future attempts of this kind, I directed a stage to be built on the forecastle, so that the cables should be more directly under the eye of the sentinel; and I likewise gave orders that one of the midshipmen should keep watch forward.

In the afternoon, Oreepyah returned from Tethuroa. He told me, that Moannah and himself had narrowly escaped being lost in the bad weather, and that Moannah had been obliged to take shelter at Eimeo. Several canoes had been lost lately in their passage to or from Tethuroa. The oversetting of their canoes is not the only risk they have to encounter, but is productive of another danger more dreadful; for at such times many become a prey to the sharks, which are very numerous in these seas. I was informed likewise, that they were sometimes attacked by a fish, which, by their description, I imagine to be the barracoota, as they attribute to it the same propensity.

Saturday passed without my seeing any thing of Tinah the whole day. The next morning, he and Iddeah came to me, and assured me that they had made the strictest inquiries concerning the injury intended us, but had not been able to discover any circumstance which could lead them to suspect who were concerned in it. This was not at all satisfactory, and I behaved towards them with great coolness, at which they were much distressed; and Iddeah, at length, gave

vent to her sorrow by tears. I could no longer keep up the appearance of mistrusting them; but I earnestly recommended to them, as they valued the King of England's friendship, that they would exert their utmost endeavours to find out the offenders; which they faithfully promised. Our reconciliation accordingly took place, and messengers were sent to acquaint Otow and Teppahoo, and to invite them to return.

It has since occurred to me, that this attempt to cut the ship adrift, was most probably the act of some of our own people; whose purpose of remaining at Otaheite might have been effectually answered, without danger, if the ship had been driven on shore. At the time, I entertained not the least thought of this kind, nor did the possibility of it enter into my ideas, having no suspicion that so general an inclination, or so strong an attachment to these islands, could prevail among my people, as to induce them to abandon every prospect of returning to their native country.

A messenger came to me this afternoon, from the Earee of Tiarraboo, the S. E. division of Otaheite, with an invitation for me to visit him. I excused myself on account of the distance, and, at Tinah's request, sent back by the messenger a handsome present, which I hope Tinah will get the credit of. I observed, with much satisfaction, that a great part of what Tinah had received from me, he had distributed; to some, out of friendship and esteem, and to others, from motives of political civility.

Tuesday, 10th.—Teppahoo and his family left us to-day to go to Tettaha, where a grand heiva was to be performed, at which their presence was required.

Wednesday, 11th.—A small party of heiva people passed through Oparre this morning, in their way to Tettaha, where they were going by appointment. They had the civility to send me word, that, if I chose, they would stay to perform a short heiva before me; and I immediately attended. It began by a dance of two young girls, to the music of drums and flutes, which lasted no long time; at the conclusion, they suddenly dropped all their dress, which was left as a present for me, and went off without my seeing them any more. After this, the men danced: their performance was more indecent than any I had before seen, but was not the less applauded on that account by the natives, who seemed much delighted.

After this entertainment, I went with Tinah and Iddeah, to pay a visit to an old lady named Wanow-oora, widow to Towah, the late Earee of Tettaha, who conducted the expedition against Eimeo, when Captain Cook was here in 1777. The old lady had just landed, and we found her sitting on the beach, by the head of her canoe. With Tinah was a priest and three men, who carried a young dog, a fowl, and two young plantain boughs; these were intended for the offering, or present, called Otee. Tinah and his party seated themselves at about ten yards distance from Wanow-oora, and were addressed by her in short sentences, for a few minutes, and received her Otee, which was exactly the same as his. Tinah's priest, in return, made a short prayer, and his offering was presented to the old lady. Tinah then rose, and went to her, and embraced her in a very affectionate manner; and she returned his kindness with tears, and many expressions which I could not understand. Soon after he conducted her to a shed, and we remained with her till it was time to go on board to dinner. I invited her to be of the party, but she excused herself on account of age and infirmity. Tinah gave directions for her and her attendants to be supplied with whatever they had occasion for, and we went off to the ship.

Friday, the 13th.—This forenoon Tinah sent to inform me, that many strangers were arrived from all parts, to be present at a grand heiva, which he had prepared in compliment to me. I accordingly went on shore, and found a great crowd of people collected together. A ring was made at a little distance from our post, and Tinah and several other chiefs came to meet me. When we were all seated, the heiva began by women dancing; after which a present of cloth, and a tawme or breast-plate, was laid before me. This ceremony being over, the men began to wrestle, and regularity was no longer preserved. Old Otow came to me, and desired I would help to put a stop to the wrestling, as the people came from different districts, some of which were ill-disposed towards others. What Otow had apprehended was not without reason, for in an instant the whole was tumult: every man took to his arms, and, as I found my single interference could be of no service, I retired to our post, and ordered all my people there under arms. At the time the disturbance began, Tinah and Iddeah were absent: their first care was for me, and Iddeah came to see if I was safe at the post. She had a double covering of cloth round her, and her waist was girded with a large rope. I desired her to stay under my protection: this she would not consent to, but said she would return as soon as all was over; and away she went.

I immediately gave orders for two guns to be fired from the ship without shot, which had a good effect: and, as no chief was concerned in the tumult, but, on the contrary, all of them exerted their influence to prevent mischief, every thing was soon quiet, and Tinah and Iddeah returned to let me know that all was settled. They went on board, with some other chiefs, and dined with me.

After dinner, I went on shore with Tinah and his friends; and I found three large hogs dressed, and a quantity of bread-fruit, which he had ordered to be prepared before he went on board, and now desired I would present them to the different parties that had come to see the entertainment:—one to the chief people of Attahooroo, one to the Arreoys, and a third to the performers of the heiva. I presented them according to his directions, and they were received with thankfulness and pleasure. This I looked upon as very handsomely done on the part of Tinah, and I was glad to see that it was regarded in the same light by his guests. These instances of liberality make full amends for the little slips which I have formerly noticed in Tinah. At this time, a day seldom passed, that he did not give proofs of his hospitality, by entertaining the principal people that came from different parts of the island to visit him, or to see the ship. Some of the chiefs he commonly invited to dine on board, and made provision for others on shore. Scarce any person of consequence went away without receiving some present from him. This I encouraged, and was glad it

was in my power to assist him. But, besides the political motives that I have alluded to, it would be unjust to Tinah not to acknowledge that his disposition seemed improved: he was more open and unreserved in his manners than formerly, and his hospitality was natural and without ostentation.

Monday, the 16th.—I was present this afternoon, at a wrestling-match by women. The manner of challenging, and method of attack, were exactly the same as among the men. The only difference that I could observe, was not in favour of the softer sex; for in these contests they showed less temper, and more animosity than I could have imagined them capable of. The women, I was told, not only wrestle with each other, but sometimes with the men; of this I have never seen an instance, and imagine it can happen but seldom, as the women in general are small, and by no means masculine. Iddeah is said to be very famous at this exercise.

Tuesday, the 17th.—I walked with Tinah towards the hills, to see his country residence, which was at a very neat house, pleasantly situated, and surrounded with plantations. From this place we saw the island Tethuroa. The next morning, I went to Matavai, to look after the Indian corn, which I judged would be full ripe for gathering; but, on my arrival, I found that the natives had been beforehand with me, the whole being taken away. This I was not at all sorry for, as it shows that they value it too much to neglect cultivating it.

Monday, 23rd.—Iddeah sent on board, for our dinners to-day, a very fine tarro pudding; and Tinah brought a bunch of bananas, that weighed eighty-one pounds, on which were two hundred and eighty-six fine fruit: ten had broken off in the carriage. The tarro pudding is excellent eating, and easily made: I shall describe this piece of cookery, as the knowledge of it may be useful in the West Indies. The tarro being cleared of the outside skin, is grated down, and made up in rolls of about half a pound each, which they cover neatly with leaves, and bake for near half an hour. An equal quantity of ripe cocoa-nut meat is likewise grated, from which, through a strainer, the rich milky juice is expressed. This juice is heated, by putting smooth hot stones in the vessel that contains it, and the tarro is then mixed with it, and kept constantly stirring to prevent burning, till it is ready, which is known by the cocoa-nut juice turning to a clear oil.

Wednesday, 25th.—Iddeah was very uneasy to-day, on account of her youngest child being ill. She would not accept of assistance from our surgeon, but said she had sent to Tettaha for a man, who she expected would come and tell her what to do. These physical people are called *Tata rapaow*.

Thursday, 26th.—This morning, a man died of a consumption, about two miles from our post. I was informed of it by Mr. Peckover, the gunner, who I had desired to look out for such a circumstance. I therefore went, accompanied by Iddeah, in hopes of seeing the funeral ceremony; but before we arrived, the body was removed to the Toopapow. It lay bare, except a piece of cloth round the loins, and another round the neck: the eyes were closed: the hands were placed, one over the pit of the stomach, and the other upon his breast. On a finger of each hand was a ring, made of platted fibres of the cocoa-nut tree, with a small bunch of red feathers. Under the Toopa-

D

any man belonging to the ship was without a *tyo*, who brought to him presents, chiefly of provisions for a sea store.

Friday, the 3rd of April.—Tinah and his wife, with his parents, brothers, and sister, dined with me to-day, and, as I meant to sail early the next morning, they all remained on board for the night. The ship was crowded the whole day with the natives, and we were loaded with cocoa-nuts, plantains, bread-fruit, hogs, and goats. In the evening, there was no dancing or mirth on the beach, such as we had been accustomed to, but all was silent.

Saturday, 4th.—At day-light, we unmoored: the stock of the best bower anchor was so much eaten by the worms, that it broke in stowing the anchor: the small bower had an iron stock ; and in these voyages, it is very necessary that ships should be provided with iron anchor-stocks. At half past six, there being no wind, we weighed, and, with our boats and two sweeps, towed the ship out of the harbour. Soon after, the sea breeze came, and we stood off towards the sea.

The outlet of Toahroah harbour being narrow, I could permit only a few of the natives to be on board: many others, however, attended in canoes, till the breeze came, when I was obliged to leave them. We stood off and on, almost all the remainder of the day. Tinah and Iddeah pressed me very strongly to anchor in Matavai bay, and stay one night longer ; but, as I had already taken leave of most of my friends, I thought it better to keep to my intention of sailing. After dinner, I ordered the presents which I had reserved for Tinah and his wife, to be put in one of the ship's boats, and, as I had promised him fire-arms, I gave him two muskets, a pair of pistols, and a good stock of ammunition. I then represented to them, the necessity of their going away, that the boat might return to the ship before it was dark ; on which they took a most affectionate leave of me, and went into the boat. One of their expressions, at parting, was " *Yourah no t' Eatua tea esserah*," "May the Eatua protect you, for ever and ever."

All the time that we remained at Otaheite, the picture of Captain Cook, at the desire of Tinah, was kept on board the ship. On delivering it to him, I wrote on the back, the time of the ship's arrival and departure, with an account of the number of plants on board.

Tinah had desired that I would salute him, at his departure, with the great guns, which I could not comply with, for fear of disturbing the plants ; but, as a parting token of our regard, we manned ship with all hands, and gave him three cheers. At sunset, the boat returned, and we made sail, bidding farewell to Otaheite, where for twenty-three weeks we had been treated with the utmost affection and regard, and which seemed to increase in proportion to our stay. That we were not insensible to their kindness, the events which followed more than sufficiently prove : for to the friendly and endearing behaviour of these people, may be ascribed the motives for that event which effected the ruin of an expedition, that there was every reason to hope, would have been completed in the most fortunate manner.

To enter into a description of the island, or its inhabitants, I look upon as superfluous. From the accounts of former voyages, and the facts which I have related, the character of the people will appear in as true a light, as by any description in my power to give. The length of time that we remained at Otaheite, with the advantage of having been there before, gave me opportunities of making, perhaps, a more perfect vocabulary of the language, than has yet appeared ; but I have chosen to defer it for the present, as there is a probability that I may hereafter be better qualified for such a task.

CHAPTER XII.

AT THE ISLAND HUAHEINE—A FRIEND OF OMAI VISITS THE SHIP—LEAVE THE SOCIETY ISLANDS—A WATER-SPOUT—THE ISLAND WHYTOOTACKEE DISCOVERED—ANCHOR IN ANNAMOOKA ROAD—OUR PARTIES ON SHORE ROBBED BY THE NATIVES—SAIL FROM ANNAMOOKA—THE CHIEFS DETAINED ON BOARD—PART FRIENDLY.

SUNDAY, 5th April 1789.—We steered towards the Island Huaheine, which we got sight of the next morning. At noon we brought to, near the entrance of Owharre harbour, it not being my intention to anchor. We could see every part of the harbour distinctly, but my attention was particularly directed to the spot where Omai's house had stood, no part of which was now visible. It was near three o'clock before any canoes came off to us, for the people on shore imagined that the ship was coming into the harbour. The first that arrived, had three men in it, who brought a few cocoa-nuts. I enquired about the chief, or *Earee Rahie* ; and one of the fellows, with great gravity, said, he was the *Earee Rahie*, and that he had come to desire I would bring the ship into the harbour. I could not help laughing at his impudence : however, I gave him a few nails for his cocoa-nuts, and he left us. Immediately after, a double canoe, in which were ten men, came alongside ; among them was a young man, who recollected and called me by my name. Several other canoes arrived, with hogs, yams, and other provisions, which we purchased. My acquaintance told me that he had lived with our friend Omai. He confirmed the account that has already been given ; and informed me, that, of all the animals which had been left with Omai, the mare only remained alive. He said that Omai and himself had often rode together ; and I observed, that many of the islanders, who came on board, had the representation of a man on horseback tattowed on their legs. After the death of Omai, his house was broken to pieces, and the materials stolen. The fire-arms were at Ulietea, but useless. I enquired after the seeds and plants, and was informed that they were all destroyed, except one tree ; but of what kind that was, I could not make out from their description. I was much pressed to take the ship into the harbour, and Omai's companion requested me to let him go to England. When they found that I would not stop among them, they seemed jealous of our going to Ulietea, and it appeared to give them some satisfaction, when I told them that I should not go near that island.

The canoes had left us, and we were making sail, when we discovered an Indian in the water, swimming towards the shore, which in all probability he would not have been able to reach. We took him up, and, luckily, another canoe coming alongside, we put him in her. The people of the canoe said that the man was insane; but how he came to be swimming so far from the land, we could not conjecture. At six o'clock we made sail, and ran all night to the S.W., and S.W. by S., between the Islands Huaheine and Ulietea. The next morning, I altered the course, steering more to the westward, for the Friendly Islands.

On the 9th, at nine o'clock in the morning, the weather became squally, and a body of thick black clouds collected in the east. Soon after, a water-spout was seen at no great distance from us, which appeared to great advantage from the darkness of the clouds behind it. As nearly as I could judge, it was about two feet diameter at the upper part, and about eight inches at the lower. I had scarce made these remarks, when I observed that it was advancing rapidly towards the ship. We immediately altered our course, and took in all the sails, except the foresail; soon after which, it passed within ten yards of our stern, making a rustling noise, but without our feeling the least effect from its being so near us. The rate at which it travelled I judged to be about ten miles per hour, going towards the west in the direction of the wind. In a quarter of an hour after passing us, it dispersed. I never was so near a water-spout before: the connection between the column, which was higher than our mast-heads, and the water below, was no otherwise visible, than by the sea being disturbed in a circular space of about six yards in diameter, the centre of which, from the whirling of the water round it, formed a hollow; and from the outer parts of the circle, the water was thrown up with much force, in a spiral direction, and could be traced to the height of fifteen or twenty feet. At this elevation we lost sight of it, and could see nothing of its junction with the column above. It is impossible to say what injury we should have suffered, if it had passed directly over us. Masts, I imagine, might have been carried away, but I do not apprehend it would have endangered the loss of a ship.

As we sailed very near the track made in former voyages, I had little reason to expect that we should at this time make any new discovery; nevertheless, on the 11th, at day-light, land was seen to the S.S.W., at about five leagues' distance, which appeared to be an island of a moderate height. On the north part was a round hill: the N.W. part was highest and steep: the S.E. part sloped off to a low point.

The wind had been westerly since the pre-ceding noon, and at the time we saw the land, the ship was standing to the N.W. At six, we tacked to the southward, and, as we advanced in that direction, discovered a number of low keys, of which at noon we counted nine: they were all covered with trees. The large island first seen had a most fruitful appearance, its shore being bordered with flat land, on which grew innumerable cocoa-nut and other trees; and the higher grounds beautifully interspersed with lawns. The wind being light and unfavourable, we endeavoured all day, but without success, to get near the land. In the night we had a heavy squall, which obliged us to clew up all our sails, and soon after it fell calm.

On the 12th, the winds were light and variable all day, with calms. At two in the afternoon, we were within three miles of the southernmost key, and could see a number of people within the reefs. Shortly after, a canoe, in which were four men, paddled off to us, and came alongside, without showing any signs of apprehension or surprise. I gave them a few beads, and they came into the ship. One man, who seemed to have an ascend-ancy over the others, looked about the ship with some appearance of curiosity, but none of them would venture to go below. They asked for some boiled fresh pork, which they saw in a bowl, belonging to one of the seamen, and it was given them to eat, with boiled plantains. Being told that I was the *Earee* or chief of the ship, the principal person came and joined noses with me, and presented to me a large mother-of-pearl shell, which hung with platted hair round his neck; this he fastened round my neck, with signs of great satisfaction.

They spoke the same language as at Otaheite, with very little variation, as far as I could judge. In a small vocabulary, that I made whilst con-versing with these men, only four words, out of twenty-four, differed from the Otaheite. The name of the large island, they told me, was Wytootackee, and the Earee was called Lomakkayah. They said that there were no hogs, dogs, or goats upon the island, nor had they yams, or tarro; but that plantains, cocoa-nuts, fowls, bread-fruit, and avees, were there in great abundance. Notwithstanding they said that no hogs were on the island, it was evident they had seen such animals; for they called them by the same name as is given to them at Otaheite, which made me suspect that they were deceiving me. However, I ordered a young boar and sow to be put into their canoe, with some yams and tarro, as we could afford to part with some of these articles. I also gave to each of them a knife, a small adze, some nails, beads, and a looking-glass. The latter they examined with great curiosity; but with the iron-work they appeared to be acquainted; calling it *aouree*, which is the common name for iron among the islands where it is known.

As they were preparing to leave us, the chief of the canoe took possession of every thing that I had given to the others. One of them showed some signs of dissatisfaction; but, after a little altercation, they joined noses, and were recon-ciled. I now thought they were going to leave the ship; but only two of them went into the canoe, the other two purposing to stay all night with us, and to have the canoe return for them in the morning. I would have treated their confi-dence with the regard it merited, but it was im-possible to say how far the ship might be driven from the island in the night. This I explained to them, and they reluctantly consented to leave us. They were very solicitous that somebody from the ship should go on shore with them; and just before they quitted us, they gave me a wooden spear, which was the only thing, the paddles excepted, they had brought with them in the canoe. It was a common long staff, pointed with the *toa* wood.

The people that came off to us did not differ in appearance from the natives of Hervey's Islands, seen in Captain Cook's last voyage, though much more friendly and inoffensive in their manners. They were tattowed across the arms and legs, but not on the loins or posteriors, like the people of

Otaheite. From their knowledge of iron, they have doubtless communication with Hervey's Islands, which are not more than eighteen leagues distant from them.

In the night, a breeze sprung up from the south, and we continued our course to the westward.

On the 18th, at sunset, we saw Savage Island; and in the night, passed by to the southward of it.

At eleven o'clock in the forenoon of the 21st, we saw the island Caow, from the mast-head, bearing N.W. by W. ½ W. This island is a high mountain, with a sharp-pointed top, and is the northwesternmost of all the Friendly Islands. At noon we saw it very distinctly from the deck, it being three leagues distant from us.

The wind being to the southward, we could not fetch Annamooka, at which island I intended to stop, before the evening of the 23rd, when we anchored in the road, in twenty-three fathoms; the extremes of Annamooka bearing E. by N. and S. by E., our distance from the shore being half a league. In the middle of the day, a canoe had come off to us from the island Mango, in which was a chief, named Latoomy-lange, who dined with me. Immediately on our anchoring, several canoes came alongside, with yams and cocoa-nuts, but none of the natives offered to come on board, without first asking permission. As yet, I had seen no person with whom I could recollect to have been formerly acquainted. I made enquiries after some of our old friends, particularly the chiefs, but I found myself not sufficiently master of the language to obtain the information I wanted.

Friday, 24th.—Our station being inconvenient for watering, at daylight we weighed, and worked more to the eastward, where we anchored in twenty-one fathoms; our distance from the shore being half a league. Sounded all round the ship, and found the ground to be a coarse coral bottom, but with even soundings.

By this time, some large sailing canoes were arrived from different islands in the neighbourhood of Annamooka; and an old lame man, named Tepa, whom I had known in 1777, and immediately recollected, came on board. Two other chiefs, whose names were Noocaboo and Kunócappo, were with him. Tepa having formerly been accustomed to our manner of speaking their language, I found I could converse with him tolerably well. He informed me, that Poulaho, Feenow, and Tubow, were alive, and at Tongataboo, and that they would come hither as soon as they heard of our arrival, of which he promised to send them immediate notice. He said that the cattle which we had left at Tongataboo had all bred, and that the old ones were yet living. He enquired after several people who were here with Captain Cook. Being desirous to see the ship, I took him and his companions below, and showed them the bread-fruit and other plants, at seeing which they were greatly surprised. I made each of them a present; and, when they had satisfied their curiosity, I invited them to go on shore with me in the ship's boat.

I took Nelson with me to procure some bread-fruit plants, one of our stock being dead, and two or three others a little sickly. When we landed, there were about two hundred people on the beach, most of them women and children. Tepa showed me a large boat-house, which, he told me, we might make use of; thinking we should have a party on shore, as our ships had formerly. I went with him in search of water, but could find no better place than where Captain Cook had watered, which is a quarter of a mile inland from the east end of the beach. I next walked to the west point of the bay, where some plants and seeds had been sown by Captain Cook; and had the satisfaction to see, in a plantation close by, about twenty fine pine-apple plants, but no fruit, this not being the proper season. They told me, that they had eaten many of them, that they were fine and large, and that at Tongataboo there were great numbers.

When I returned to the landing-place, I was desired to sit down, and a present was brought me, which consisted of some bundles of cocoa-nuts only. This fell short of my expectations; however, I appeared satisfied, and distributed beads and trinkets to the women and children near me.

Numerous were the marks of mourning with which these people disfigure themselves, such as bloody temples, their heads deprived of most of the hair, and, what was worse, almost all of them with the loss of some of their fingers. Several fine boys, not above six years old, had lost both their little fingers; and some of the men, besides these, had parted with the middle finger of the right hand.

The chiefs went off with me to dinner, and I found a brisk trade carrying on at the ship for yams; some plantains and bread-fruit were likewise brought on board, but no hogs. In the afternoon, more sailing canoes arrived, some of which contained not less than ninety passengers. We purchased eight hogs, some dogs, fowls, and shaddocks. Yams were in great abundance, very fine and large; one yam weighed above forty-five pounds. Among the people that came this afternoon, were two of the name of Tubow, which is a family of the first distinction among the Friendly Islands; one of them was chief of the island Lefooga; with him and Tepa I went on shore to see the wooding-place. I found a variety of sizable trees; but the kind which I principally pitched upon, was the Barringtonia, of Forster. I acquainted Tepa with my intention of sending people to cut wood, which meeting with his approbation, we parted.

On the 25th, at daylight, the wooding and watering parties went on shore. I had directed them not to cut the kind of tree* which, when Captain Cook wooded here in 1777, blinded, for a time, many of the wood-cutters. They had not been an hour on shore, before one man had an axe stolen from him, and another an adze. Tepa was applied to, who got the axe restored, but the adze was not recovered. In the evening we completed wooding.

Sunday, 26th.—In the morning, Nelson went on shore to get a few plants; but, no principal chief being among the people, he was insulted, and a spade taken from him. A boat's grapnel was likewise stolen from the watering party.

* *Excoecaria Agallocha Linn. Sp. Pl.*, called in the Malay language, *Cayu Mata Boota*, which signifies, the tree that wounds the eyes.

Tepa recovered the spade for us; but the crowd of natives was become so great, by the number of canoes that had arrived from different islands, that it was impossible to do anything, where there was such a multitude of people, without a chief of sufficient authority to command the whole. I therefore ordered the watering party to go on board, and determined to sail; for I could not discover that any canoe had been sent to acquaint the chiefs of Tongataboo of our being here. For some time after the thefts were committed, the chiefs kept away, but before noon, they came on board.

At noon, we unmoored, and at one o'clock, got under sail. The two Tubows, Kunocappo, Latoomy-lange, and another chief, were on board, and I acquainted them that, unless the grapnel was returned, they must remain in the ship. They were surprised, and not a little alarmed. Canoes were immediately dispatched after the grapnel, which, I was informed, could not possibly be brought to the ship before the next day, as those who had stolen it immediately sailed with their prize to another island. Nevertheless, I detained them till sunset, when their uneasiness and impatience increased to such a degree, that they began to beat themselves about the face and eyes, and some of them cried bitterly. As this distress was more than the grapnel was worth, and I had no reason to imagine that they were privy to, or in any manner concerned in the theft, I could not think of detaining them longer, and called their canoes alongside. I then told them they were at liberty to go, and made each of them a present of a hatchet, a saw, with some knives, gimblets, and nails. This unexpected present, and the sudden change in their situation, affected them not less with joy than they had before been with apprehension. They were unbounded in their acknowledgments; and I have little doubt but that we parted better friends than if the affair had never happened.

We stood to the northward all night, with light winds, and on the next day, the 27th, at noon, were between the islands Tofoa and Kotoo. Latitude observed 19° 18′ S.

Thus far the voyage had advanced in a course of uninterrupted prosperity, and had been attended with many circumstances equally pleasing and satisfactory. A very different scene was now to be experienced. A conspiracy had been formed, which was to render all our past labour productive only of extreme misery and distress. The means had been concerted and prepared with so much secrecy and circumspection, that no one circumstance appeared to occasion the smallest suspicion of the impending calamity.

CHAPTER XIII.

A MUTINY IN THE SHIP.

MONDAY, 27th April, 1789.—We kept near the island Kotoo all the afternoon, in hopes that some canoes would come off to the ship; but in this I was disappointed. The wind being northerly in the evening, we steered to the westward, to pass to the south of Tofoa. I gave directions for this course to be continued during the night. The master had the first watch, the gunner the middle watch, and Mr. Christian the morning watch. This was the turn of duty for the night.

Tuesday, 28th.—Just before sun-rising, while I was yet asleep, Mr. Christian, with the master-at-arms, gunner's mate, and Thomas Burkitt, seaman, came into my cabin, and, seizing me, tied my hands with a cord behind my back, threatening me with instant death if I spoke or made the least noise. I, however, called as loud as I could in hopes of assistance; but they had already secured the officers who were not of their party, by placing sentinels at their doors. There were three men at my cabin door, besides the four within; Christian had only a cutlass in his hand, the others had muskets and bayonets. I was hauled out of bed and forced on deck in my shirt, suffering great pain from the tightness with which they had tied my hands. I demanded the reason of such violence, but received no other answer than abuse for not holding my tongue. The master, the gunner, the surgeon, Mr. Elphinstone, master's mate, and Nelson, were kept confined below, and the fore-hatchway was guarded by sentinels. The boatswain and carpenter, and also the clerk, Mr. Samuel, were allowed to come upon deck, where they saw me standing abaft the mizen-mast, with my hands tied behind my back, under a guard, with Christian at their head. The boatswain was ordered to hoist the launch out, with a threat, if he did not do it instantly, *to take care of himself.*

When the boat was out, Mr. Hayward and Mr. Hallet, two of the midshipmen, and Mr. Samuel, were ordered into it. I demanded what their intention was in giving this order, and endeavoured to persuade the people near me not to persist in such acts of violence; but it was to no effect, "Hold your tongue, sir, or you are dead this instant," was constantly repeated to me.

The master by this time had sent to request that he might come on deck, which was permitted; but he was soon ordered back again to his cabin.

I continued my endeavours to turn the tide of affairs, when Christian changed the cutlass which he had in his hand for a bayonet that was brought to him, and, holding me with a strong gripe by the cord that tied my hands, he with many oaths threatened to kill me immediately, if I would not be quiet; the villains round me had their pieces cocked and bayonets fixed. Particular people were called on to go into the boat, and were hurried over the side, whence I concluded that with these people I was to be set adrift. I therefore made another effort to bring about a change, but with no other effect than to be threatened with having my brains blown out.

The boatswain and seamen who were to go in the boat were allowed to collect twine, canvas, lines, sails, cordage, an eight-and-twenty gallon cask of water, and Mr. Samuel got 150 pounds of bread, with a small quantity of rum and wine, also a quadrant and compass; but he was forbidden, on pain of death, to touch either map, ephemeris, book of astronomical observations, sextant, time-keeper, or any of my surveys or drawings.

The mutineers having forced those of the seamen whom they meant to get rid of into the boat, Christian directed a dram to be served to each of his own crew. I then unhappily saw that nothing could be done to effect the recovery of the ship;

there was no one to assist me, and every endeavour on my part was answered with threats of death.

The officers were next called upon deck and forced over the side into the boat, while I was kept apart from every one abaft the mizen-mast, Christian, armed with a bayonet, holding me by the bandage that secured my hands. The guard round me had their pieces cocked, but on my daring the ungrateful wretches to fire, they uncocked them.

Isaac Martin, one of the guard over me, I saw had an inclination to assist me, and as he fed me with shaddock (my lips being quite parched), we explained our wishes to each other by our looks; but this being observed, Martin was removed from me. He then attempted to leave the ship, for which purpose he got into the boat; but with many threats they obliged him to return.

The armourer, Joseph Coleman, and two of the carpenters, M'Intosh and Norman, were also kept contrary to their inclination; and they begged of me, after I was astern in the boat, to remember that they declared they had no hand in the transaction. Michael Byrne, I am told, likewise wanted to leave the ship.

It is of no moment for me to recount my endeavours to bring back the offenders to a sense of their duty; all I could do was by speaking to them in general; but it was to no purpose, for I was kept securely bound, and no one except the guard suffered to come near me.

To Mr. Samuel I am indebted for securing my journals and commission, with some material ship papers. Without these I had nothing to certify what I had done, and my honour and character might have been suspected, without my possessing a proper document to have defended them. All this he did with great resolution, though guarded and strictly watched. He attempted to save the time-keeper, and a box with my surveys, drawings, and remarks for fifteen years past, which were numerous, when he was hurried away, with "Damn your eyes, you are well off to get what you have."

It appeared to me, that Christian was some time in doubt whether he should keep the carpenter or his mates; at length he determined on the latter, and the carpenter was ordered into the boat. He was permitted, but not without some opposition, to take his tool-chest.

Much altercation took place among the mutinous crew during the whole business: some swore "I'll be damned if he does not find his way home, if he gets anything with him," (meaning me); and, when the carpenter's chest was carrying away, "Damn my eyes, he will have a vessel built in a month;" while others laughed at the helpless situation of the boat, being very deep, and so little room for those who were in her. As for Christian, he seemed as if meditating destruction on himself and every one else.

I asked for arms, but they laughed at me, and said I was well acquainted with the people among whom I was going, and therefore did not want them; four cutlasses, however, were thrown into the boat after we were veered astern.

The officers and men being in the boat, they only waited for me, of which the master-at-arms informed Christian; who then said—"Come, Captain Bligh, your officers and men are now in the boat, and you must go with them; if you attempt to make the least resistance you will instantly be put to death:" and, without further ceremony, with a tribe of armed ruffians about me, I was forced over the side, where they untied my hands. Being in the boat, we were veered astern by a rope. A few pieces of pork were thrown to us, and some clothes, also the cutlasses I have already mentioned; and it was then that the armourer and carpenters called out to me to remember that they had no hand in the transaction. After having undergone a great deal of ridicule, and been kept some time to make sport for these unfeeling wretches, we were at length cast adrift in the open ocean.

I had with me in the boat the following persons:

Names.	Stations.
JOHN FRYER	Master.
THOMAS LEDWARD	Acting Surgeon.
DAVID NELSON	Botanist.
WILLIAM PECKOVER	Gunner.
WILLIAM COLE	Boatswain.
WILLIAM PURCELL	Carpenter.
WILLIAM ELPHINSTONE	Master's Mate.
THOMAS HAYWARD	Midshipmen.
JOHN HALLET	
JOHN NORTON	Quarter Masters.
PETER LINKLETTER	
LAWRENCE LEBOGUE	Sailmaker.
JOHN SMITH	Cooks.
THOMAS HALL	
GEORGE SIMPSON	Quarter Master's Mate.
ROBERT TINKLER	A Boy.
ROBERT LAMB	Butcher.
MR. SAMUEL	Clerk.

There remained on board the Bounty:

FLETCHER CHRISTIAN	Master's Mate.
PETER HEYWOOD	Midshipmen.
EDWARD YOUNG	
GEORGE STEWART	
CHARLES CHURCHILL	Master at Arms.
JOHN MILLS	Gunner's Mate.
JAMES MORRISON	Boatswain's Mate.
THOMAS BURKITT	Able Seaman.
MATTHEW QUINTAL	Ditto.
JOHN SUMNER	Ditto.
JOHN MILLWARD	Ditto.
WILLIAM M'KOY	Ditto.
HENRY HILLBRANT	Ditto.
MICHAEL BYRNE	Ditto.
WILLIAM MUSPRAT	Ditto.
ALEXANDER SMITH	Ditto.
JOHN WILLIAMS	Ditto.
THOMAS ELLISON	Ditto.
ISAAC MARTIN	Ditto.
RICHARD SKINNER	Ditto.
MATTHEW THOMPSON	Ditto.
WILLIAM BROWN	Gardener.
JOSEPH COLEMAN	Armourer.
CHARLES NORMAN	Carpenter's Mate.
THOMAS M'INTOSH	Carpenter's Crew.

In all twenty-five hands, and the most able men of the ship's company.

Having little or no wind, we rowed pretty fast towards Tofoa, which bore N. E. about ten leagues from us. While the ship was in sight, she steered to the W.N.W., but I considered this only as a feint; for when we were sent away—"Huzza for Otaheite," was frequently heard among the mutineers.

Christian, the chief of the mutineers, was of a respectable family in the north of England. This was the third voyage he had made with me; and as I found it necessary to keep my ship's company at three watches, I had given him an order to take charge of the third, his abilities being thoroughly equal to the task; and by this means the master and gunner were not at watch and watch.

Heywood * was also of a respectable family in the north of England, and a young man of abilities, as well as Christian. These two had been objects of my particular regard and attention, and I had taken great pains to instruct them, having entertained hopes, that as professional men, they would have become a credit to their country.

Young was well recommended, and had the look of an able stout seaman; he, however, fell short of what his appearance promised.

Stewart was a young man of creditable parents, in the Orkneys; at which place, on the return of the Resolution from the South Seas, in 1780, we received so many civilities, that, on that account only, I should gladly have taken him with me; but, independent of this recommendation, he was a seaman, and had always borne a good character.

Notwithstanding the roughness with which I was treated, the remembrance of past kindnesses produced some signs of remorse in Christian. When they were forcing me out of the ship, I asked him, if this treatment was a proper return for the many instances he had received of my friendship? he appeared disturbed at my question, and answered with much emotion, "That,—Captain Bligh, —that is the thing ;—I am in hell—I am in hell."

As soon as I had time to reflect, I felt an inward satisfaction, which prevented any depression of my spirits: conscious of my integrity, and anxious solicitude for the good of the service in which I had been engaged, I found my mind wonderfully supported, and I began to conceive hopes, notwithstanding so heavy a calamity, that I should one day be able to account to my King and my country for the misfortune.—A few hours before, my situation had been peculiarly flattering. I had a ship in the most perfect order, and well stored with every necessary both for service and health: by early attention to those particulars I had, as much as lay in my power, provided against any accident in case I could not get through Endeavour Straits, as well as against what might befal me in them; add to this, the plants had been successfully preserved in the most flourishing state: so that upon the whole, the voyage was two thirds completed, and the remaining part, to all appearance, in a very promising way; every person on board being in perfect health, to establish which was ever amongst the principal objects of my attention.

It will very naturally be asked, what could be the reason for such a revolt? in answer to which I can only conjecture, that the mutineers had flattered themselves with the hopes of a more happy life among the Otaheiteans, than they could possibly enjoy in England; and this, joined to some female connexions, most probably occasioned the whole transaction.

The women at Otaheite are handsome, mild and cheerful in their manners and conversation, possessed of great sensibility, and have sufficient delicacy to make them admired and beloved. The chiefs were so much attached to our people, that

they rather encouraged their stay among them than otherwise, and even made them promises of large possessions. Under these, and many other attendant circumstances, equally desirable, it is now perhaps not so much to be wondered at, though scarcely possible to have been foreseen, that a set of sailors, most of them void of connexions, should be led away: especially when, in addition to such powerful inducements, they imagined it in their power to fix themselves in the midst of plenty, on one of the finest islands in the world, where they need not labour, and where the allurements of dissipation are beyond anything that can be conceived. The utmost, however, that any commander could have supposed to have happened is, that some of the people would have been tempted to desert. But if it should be asserted, that a commander is to guard against an act of mutiny and piracy in his own ship, more than by the common rules of service, it is as much as to say that he must sleep locked up, and when awake, be girded with pistols.

Desertions have happened, more or less, from most of the ships that have been at the Society Islands; but it has always been in the commander's power to make the chiefs return their people: the knowledge, therefore, that it was unsafe to desert, perhaps, first led nine to consider with what ease so small a ship might be surprised, and that so favourable an opportunity would never offer to them again.

The secrecy of this mutiny is beyond all conception†. Thirteen of the party, who were with me, had always lived forward among the seamen; yet neither they, nor the messmates of Christian, Stewart, Heywood and Young, had ever observed any circumstance that made them in the least suspect what was going on. To such a close-planned act of villany, my mind being entirely free from any suspicion, it is not wonderful that I fell a sacrifice. Perhaps, if there had been marines on board, a sentinel at my cabin-door might have prevented it; for I slept with the door always open, that the officer of the watch might have access to me on all occasions, the possibility of such a conspiracy being ever the farthest from my thoughts. Had their mutiny been occasioned by any grievances, either real or imaginary, I must have discovered symptoms of their discontent, which would have put me on my guard: but the case was far otherwise. Christian, in particular, I was on the most friendly terms with: that very day he was engaged to have dined with me; and the preceding night, he excused himself from supping with me on pretence of being unwell; for which I felt concerned, having no suspicions of his integrity and honour.

* See Appendix.

† From subsequent disclosures it does not appear that any conspiracy had been entered into, but that the mutiny was solely occasioned by a sudden determination taken by Christian, who had received insulting language from Captain Bligh on several occasions, and particularly on the previous afternoon, and he was but too readily seconded by many of the people, particularly the men who had deserted at Otaheite. The motives which Captain Bligh ascribes to the crew generally, without doubt actuated many when the explosion occurred, but there is no reason to believe that any previous intention of mutiny existed. Heywood and Stewart, who were left behind, took no part in the affair. See Appendix.

CHAPTER XIV.

PROCEED IN THE LAUNCH TO THE ISLAND TOFOA—DIFFI-
CULTY IN OBTAINING SUPPLIES THERE—TREACHEROUS
ATTACK OF THE NATIVES—ESCAPE TO SEA, AND BEAR
AWAY FOR NEW HOLLAND.

My first determination was to seek a supply of
bread-fruit and water at Tofoa, and afterwards to
sail for Tongataboo, and there risk a solicitation
to Poulaho, the king, to equip our boat, and grant
us a supply of water and provisions, so as to enable
us to reach the East Indies.

The quantity of provisions I found in the boat,
was 150lb. of bread, 16 pieces of pork, each piece
weighing 2lb., 6 quarts of rum, 6 bottles of wine,
with 28 gallons of water, and four empty barrecoes.

Fortunately it was calm all the afternoon, till
about four o'clock, when we were so far to windward, that, with a moderate easterly breeze which
sprung up, we were able to sail. It was nevertheless dark when we got to Tofoa, where I expected to land; but the shore proved to be so
steep and rocky, that we were obliged to give up
all thoughts of it, and keep the boat under the lee
of the island with two oars; for there was no
anchorage. Having fixed on this mode of proceeding for the night, I served to every person
half a pint of grog, and each took to his rest as well
as our unhappy situation would allow.

Wednesday, April 29th.—In the morning, at dawn
of day, we rowed along shore in search of a landing-
place, and about ten o'clock we discovered a cove with
a stony beach, at the N.W. part of the island, where I
dropt the grapnel within twenty yards of the rocks.
A great surf ran on the shore; but, as I was unwil-
ling to diminish our stock of provisions, I landed
Mr. Samuel, and some others, who climbed the
cliffs and got into the country to search for supplies. The rest of us remained at the cove, not
discovering any other way into the country, than
that by which Mr. Samuel had proceeded. It was
great consolation to me to find, that the spirits of
my people did not sink, notwithstanding our
miserable and almost hopeless situation. Towards
noon, Mr. Samuel returned, with a few quarts of
water which he had found in holes; but he had
met with no spring, or any prospect of a sufficient supply in that particular, and had seen
only the signs of inhabitants. As it was uncertain
what might be our future necessities, I only issued
a morsel of bread, and a glass of wine, to each
person for dinner.

I observed the latitude of this cove to be 19°
41′ S. This is the N.W. part of Tofoa, the north-
westernmost of the Friendly Islands.

The weather was fair, but the wind blew so
strong from the E.S.E., that we could not venture
to sea. Our detention made it absolutely necessary to endeavour to obtain something towards
our support; for I determined, if possible, to keep
our first stock entire. We therefore weighed,
and rowed along shore to see if anything could
be got; and at last discovered some cocoa-nut
trees; but they were on the top of high precipices,
and the surf made it dangerous landing: both
one and the other, we however got the better of.
Some of the people, with much difficulty, climbed
the cliffs, and got about twenty cocoa-nuts, and
others slung them to ropes, by which we hauled
them through the surf into the boat. This was

all that could be done here; and, as I found no
place so safe as the one we had left, to spend the
night at, I returned to the cove, and, having
served a cocoa-nut to each person, we went to rest
again in the boat.

Thursday, 30th.—At daylight, we attempted to
put to sea; but the wind and weather proved so bad,
that I was glad to return to our former station;
where, after issuing a morsel of bread and a spoonful of rum to each person, we landed, and I went
off with Mr. Nelson, Mr. Samuel, and some others,
into the country, having hauled ourselves up the
precipice by long vines, which were fixed there
by the natives for that purpose; this being the
only way into the country.

We found a few deserted huts, and a small plantain walk, but little taken care of; from which we
could only collect three small bunches of plantains.
After passing this place, we came to a deep gully
that led towards a mountain, near a volcano; and,
as I conceived that in the rainy season very
great torrents of water must pass through it, we
hoped to find sufficient for our use remaining
in some holes of the rocks; but, after all our
search, the whole that we collected was only nine
gallons. We advanced within two miles of the
foot of the highest mountain in the island, on
which is the volcano that is almost constantly
burning. The country near it is covered with
lava, and has a most dreary appearance. As we
had not been fortunate in our discoveries, and
saw nothing to alleviate our distresses, except the
plantains and water abovementioned, we returned
to the boat, exceedingly fatigued and faint. When
I came to the precipice whence we were to
descend into the cove, I was seized with such a
dizziness in my head, that I thought it scarce possible to effect it: however, by the assistance of
Nelson and others, they at last got me down, in a
weak condition. Every person being returned by
noon, I gave about an ounce of pork and two
plantains to each, with half a glass of wine. I
again observed the latitude of this place 19°
41′ south. The people who remained by the
boat I had directed to look for fish, or what they
could pick up about the rocks; but nothing eatable could be found: so that, upon the whole, we
considered ourselves on as miserable a spot of
land as could well be imagined.

I could not say positively, from the former knowledge I had of this island, whether it was inhabited
or not; but I knew it was considered inferior to
the other islands, and I was not certain but that
the Indians only resorted to it at particular times.
I was very anxious to ascertain this point; for,
in case there had been only a few people here, and
those could have furnished us with but very
moderate supplies, the remaining in this spot to
have made preparations for our voyage, would
have been preferable to the risk of getting amongst
multitudes, where perhaps we might lose everything. A party, therefore, sufficiently strong, I
determined should go another route, as soon as the
sun became lower; and they cheerfully undertook it.

About two o'clock in the afternoon the party
set out; but, after suffering much fatigue, they returned in the evening, without any kind of success.

At the head of the cove, about 150 yards from
the water-side, there was a cave; the distance
across the stony beach was about 100 yards, and

from the country into the cove there was no other way than that which I have already described. The situation secured us from the danger of being surprised, and I determined to remain on shore for the night, with a part of my people, that the others might have more room to rest in the boat with the master; whom I directed to lie at a grapnel, and be watchful, in case we should be attacked. I ordered one plantain for each person to be boiled; and, having supped on this scanty allowance, with a quarter of a pint of grog, and fixed the watches for the night, those whose turn it was, laid down to sleep in the cave, before which we kept up a good fire; yet notwithstanding we were much troubled with flies and musquitoes.

Friday, May 1st.—At dawn of day, the party set out again in a different route, to see what they could find; in the course of which they suffered greatly for want of water: they, however, met with two men, a woman and a child: the men came with them to the cove, and brought two cocoa-nut shells of water. I endeavoured to make friends of these people, and sent them away for bread-fruit, plantains, and water. Soon after, other natives came to us; and by noon there were thirty about us, from whom we obtained a small supply; but I could only afford one ounce of pork, and a quarter of a bread-fruit to each man for dinner, with half a pint of water; for I was fixed in my resolution not to use any of the bread or water in the boat.

No particular chief was yet among the natives: they were, notwithstanding, tractable, and behaved honestly, exchanging the provisions they brought for a few buttons and beads. The party who had been out, informed me of their having seen several neat plantations; so that it remained no longer a doubt of there being settled inhabitants on the island; for which reason I determined to get what I could, and to sail the first moment that the wind and weather would allow us to put to sea.

I was much puzzled in what manner to account to the natives for the loss of my ship: I knew they had too much sense to be amused with a story that the ship was to join me, when she was not in sight from the hills. I was at first doubtful whether I should tell the real fact, or say that the ship had overset and sunk, and that we only were saved: the latter appeared to be the most proper and advantageous for us, and I accordingly instructed my people, that we might all agree in one story. As I expected, inquiries were made about the ship, and they seemed readily satisfied with our account; but there did not appear the least symptom of joy or sorrow in their faces, although I fancied I discovered some marks of surprise. Some of the natives were coming and going the whole afternoon, and we got enough of bread-fruit, plantains, and cocoa-nuts for another day; but of water they only brought us about five pints. A canoe also came in with four men, and brought a few cocoa-nuts and bread-fruit, which I bought as I had done the rest. Nails were much inquired after, but I would not suffer any to be shown, as they were wanted for the use of the boat.

Towards evening, I had the satisfaction to find our stock of provisions somewhat increased; but the natives did not appear to have much to spare. What they brought was in such small quantities,

that I had no reason to hope we should be able to procure from them sufficient to stock us for our voyage. At sun-set all the natives left us in quiet possession of the cove. I thought this a good sign, and made no doubt that they would come again the next day with a better supply of food and water, with which I hoped to sail without farther delay: for if, in attempting to get to Tongataboo, we should be driven to leeward of the islands, there would be a larger quantity of provisions to support us against such a misfortune.

At night, I served a quarter of a bread-fruit and a cocoa-nut to each person for supper; and, a good fire being made, all but the watch went to sleep.

Saturday 2nd.—At day-break, the next morning, I was pleased to find every one's spirits a little revived, and that they no longer regarded me with those anxious looks, which had constantly been directed towards me since we lost sight of the ship: every countenance appeared to have a degree of cheerfulness, and they all seemed determined to do their best.

As there was no certainty of our being supplied with water by the natives, I sent a party among the gullies in the mountains, with empty shells, to see what could be found. In their absence the natives came about us, as I expected, and in greater numbers; two canoes also came in from round the north side of the island. In one of them was an elderly chief, called Macca-ackavow. Soon after, some of our foraging party returned, and with them came a good-looking chief, called Egijeefow, or perhaps more properly Eefow, Egij or Eghee, signifying a chief. To each of these men I made a present of an old shirt and a knife, and I soon found they had either seen me, or had heard of my being at Annamooka. They knew I had been with Captain Cook, whom they inquired after, and also Captain Clerk. They were very inquisitive to know in what manner I had lost my ship. During this conversation, a young man, named Nageete, appeared, whom I remembered to have seen at Annamooka: he expressed much pleasure at our meeting. I inquired after Poulaho and Feenow, who, they said, were at Tongataboo; and Eefow agreed to accompany me thither, if I would wait till the weather moderated. The readiness and affability of this man gave me much satisfaction.

This, however, was but of short duration, for the natives began to increase in number, and I observed some symptoms of a design against us. Soon after they attempted to haul the boat on shore, on which I brandished my cutlass in a threatening manner, and spoke to Eefow to desire them to desist; which they did, and everything became quiet again. My people, who had been in the mountains, now returned with about three gallons of water. I kept buying up the little bread-fruit that was brought to us, and likewise some spears to arm my men with, having only four cutlasses, two of which were in the boat. As we had no means of improving our situation, I told our people I would wait till sun-set, by which time, perhaps, something might happen in our favour: for if we attempted to go at present, we must fight our way through, which we could do more advantageously at night; and that in the mean time we would endeavour to get off to the boat what we had bought. The beach was lined with the natives, and we heard nothing but the knocking of stones together, which they had in each hand. I knew very well this was the sign of an attack. At noon I served a cocoa-nut and a bread-fruit to each person for dinner, and gave some to the chiefs, with whom I continued to appear intimate and friendly. They frequently importuned me to sit down, but I as constantly refused: for it occurred both to Nelson and myself, that they intended to seize hold of me, if I gave them such an opportunity. Keeping, therefore, constantly on our guard, we were suffered to eat our uncomfortable meal in some quietness.

After dinner, we began by little and little to get our things into the boat, which was a troublesome business, on account of the surf. I carefully watched the motions of the natives, who continued to increase in number; and found that, instead of their intention being to leave us, fires were made, and places fixed on for their stay during the night. Consultations were also held among them, and every thing assured me we should be attacked. I sent orders to the master that when he saw us coming down he should keep the boat close to the shore, that we might the more readily embark.

I had my journal on shore with me, writing the occurrences in the cave, and in sending it down to the boat, it was nearly snatched away, but for the timely assistance of the gunner.

The sun was near setting, when I gave the word, on which every person, who was on shore with me, boldly took up his proportion of things, and carried them to the boat. The chiefs asked me if I would not stay with them all night, I said, "No, I never sleep out of my boat; but in the morning we will again trade with you, and I shall remain till the weather is moderate, that we may go, as we have agreed, to see Poulaho, at Tongataboo." Macca-ackavow then got up, and said, "You will not sleep on shore? then Mattie," (which directly signifies we will kill you) and he left me. The onset was now preparing; every one, as I have described before, kept knocking stones together, and Eefow quitted me. All but two or three things were in the boat, when I took Nageete by the hand, and we walked down the beach, every one in a silent kind of horror.

While I was seeing the people embark, Nageete wanted me to stay to speak to Eefow; but I found he was encouraging them to the attack, and it was my determination, if they had then begun, to have killed him for his treacherous behaviour. I ordered the carpenter not to quit me till the other people were in the boat. Nageete, finding I would not stay, loosed himself from my hold and went off, and we all got in the boat except one man, who while I was getting on board, quitted it, and ran up the beach to cast the sternfast off, notwithstanding the master and others called to him to return, while they were hauling me out of the water.

I was no sooner in the boat than the attack began by about two hundred men; the unfortunate poor man who had run up the beach was knocked down, and the stones flew like a shower of shot. Many Indians got hold of the stern rope, and were near hauling the boat on shore; which they would certainly have effected, if I had not had a knife in my pocket, with which I cut the rope. We then hauled off to the grapnel, every one being more or less hurt. At this time, I saw five of the natives about the poor man they had killed, and two of them were beating him about the head with stones in their hands.

We had no time to reflect, for to my surprise, they filled their canoes with stones, and twelve men came off after us, to renew the attack, which they did so effectually as nearly to disable us all. Our grapnel was foul, but Providence here assisted us; the fluke broke, and we got to our oars, and pulled to sea. They, however, could paddle round us, so that we were obliged to sustain the attack without being able to return it, except with such stones as lodged in the boat; and in this I found we were very inferior to them. We could not close, because our boat was lumbered and heavy, of which they well know how to take advantage: I therefore adopted the expedient of throwing overboard some clothes, which, as I expected, they stopped to pick up; and, as it was by this time almost dark, they gave over the attack, and returned towards the shore, leaving us to reflect on our unhappy situation.

The poor man killed by the natives was John Norton: this was his second voyage with me as a quarter-master, and his worthy character made me lament his loss very much. He has left an aged parent, I am told, whom he supported.

I once before sustained an attack of a similar nature, with a smaller number of Europeans, against a multitude of Indians: it was after the death of Captain Cook, on the Moral at Owhyhee, where I was left by Lieutenant King. Yet, notwithstanding this experience, I had not an idea that the power of a man's arm could throw stones, from two to eight pounds weight, with such force and exactness as these people did. Here unhappily we were without fire-arms, which the Indians knew; and it was a fortunate circumstance that they did not begin to attack us in the cave; for in that case our destruction must have been inevitable, and we should have had nothing left for it but to sell our lives as dearly as we could; in which I found every one cheerfully disposed to concur. This appearance of resolution deterred them, supposing they could effect their purpose without risk after we were in the boat.

Taking this as a sample of the disposition of the natives, there was but little reason to expect much benefit by persevering in the intention of visiting Poulaho; for I considered their good behaviour formerly to have proceeded from a dread of our fire-arms, and which, therefore, was likely to cease, as they knew we were now destitute of them: and, even supposing our lives not in danger, the boat and everything we had, would most probably be taken from us, and thereby all hopes precluded of ever being able to return to our native country.

We set our sails, and steered along shore by the west side of the island Tofoa; the wind blowing fresh from the eastward. My mind was employed in considering what was best to be done, when I was solicited by all hands to take them towards home: and, when I told them that no hopes of relief for us remained (except what might be found at New Holland) till I came to Timor, a distance of full twelve hundred leagues, where there was a Dutch settlement, but in what part of the island I knew not; they all agreed to live on one ounce of bread, and a quarter of a pint of water, per day.

Therefore, after examining our stock of provisions, and recommending to them, in the most solemn manner, not to depart from their promise, we bore away across a sea, where the navigation is but little known, in a small boat, twenty-three feet long from stem to stern, deep laden with eighteen men. I was happy, however, to see that every one seemed better satisfied with our situation than myself.

Our stock of provisions consisted of about one hundred and fifty pounds of bread, twenty-eight gallons of water, twenty pounds of pork, three bottles of wine, and five quarts of rum. The difference between this and the quantity we had on leaving the ship, was principally owing to our loss in the bustle and confusion of the attack. A few cocoa-nuts were in the boat, and some bread-fruit, but the latter was trampled to pieces.

CHAPTER XV.

PASSAGE TOWARDS NEW HOLLAND—ISLANDS DISCOVERED IN OUR ROUTE—OUR GREAT DISTRESSES—SEE THE REEFS OF NEW HOLLAND, AND FIND A PASSAGE THROUGH THEM.

It was about eight o'clock at night when we bore away under a reefed lug foresail; and, having divided the people into watches, and got the boat in a little order, we returned God thanks for our miraculous preservation, and, fully confident of his gracious support, I found my mind more at ease than it had been for some time past.

Sunday, 3rd.—At day-break, the gale increased; the sun rose very fiery and red, a sure indication of a severe gale of wind. At eight it blew a violent storm, and the sea ran very high, so that between the seas the sail was becalmed, and when on the top of the sea it was too much to have set: but we could not venture to take in the sail, for we were in very imminent danger and distress, the sea curling over the stern of the boat, which obliged us to bale with all our might. A situation more distressing has, perhaps, seldom been experienced.

Our bread was in bags, and in danger of being spoiled by the wet: to be starved to death was inevitable, if this could not be prevented: I therefore began to examine what clothes there were in the boat, and what other things could be spared; and, having determined that only two suits should be kept for each person, the rest was thrown overboard, with some rope and spare sails, which lightened the boat considerably, and we had more room to bale the water out. Fortunately the carpenter had a good chest in the boat, in which we secured the bread the first favourable moment. His tool chest also was cleared, and the tools stowed in the bottom of the boat, so that this became a second convenience.

I served a tea-spoonful of rum to each person, (for we were very wet and cold) with a quarter of a bread-fruit, which was scarce eatable, for dinner; our engagement was now strictly to be carried into execution, and I was fully determined to make our provisions last eight weeks, let the daily proportion be ever so small.

At noon, I considered our course and distance from Tofoa to be W.N.W. ¼ W. 86 miles, latitude 19° 27′ S. I directed the course to the W. N. W., that we might get a sight of the islands called

Feejee, if they lay in the direction the natives had pointed out to me.

The weather continued very severe, the wind veering from N.E. to E.S.E. The sea ran higher than in the forenoon, and the fatigue of baling, to keep the boat from filling, was exceedingly great. We could do nothing more than keep before the sea: in the course of which the boat performed so well, that I no longer dreaded any danger in that respect. But among the hardships we were to undergo, that of being constantly wet was not the least: the night was very cold, and at day-light on Monday, 4th, our limbs were so benumbed, that we could scarce find the use of them. At this time I served a tea-spoonful of rum to each person, from which we all found great benefit.

As I have mentioned before, I determined to keep to the W.N.W., till I got more to the northward; for I not only expected to have better weather, but to see the Feejee Islands, as I have often understood, from the natives of Annamooka, that they lie in that direction. Captain Cook likewise considered them to be N.W. by W. from Tongataboo. Just before noon, we discovered a small flat island, of a moderate height, bearing W.S.W., 4 or 5 leagues. I observed our latitude to be 18° 58′ S.; our longitude was, by account, 3° 4′ W. from the island of Tofoa, having made a N. 72° W. course, distance 95 miles, since yesterday noon. I divided five small cocoa-nuts for our dinner, and every one was satisfied.

A little after noon, other islands appeared, and at a quarter past three o'clock we could count eight, bearing from S. round by the west to N.W. by N.; those to the south, which were the nearest, being four leagues distant from us.

I kept my course to the N.W. by W., between the islands, the gale having considerably abated. At six o'clock, we discovered three other small islands to the N. W., the westernmost of them bore N.W. ½ W. 7 leagues. I steered to the southward of these islands, a W.N.W. course for the night under a reefed sail.

Served a few broken pieces of bread-fruit for supper, and performed prayers.

The night turned out fair, and, having had tolerable rest, every one seemed considerably better in the morning, Tuesday, 5th, and contentedly breakfasted on a few pieces of yams that were found in the boat. After breakfast we examined our bread, a great deal of which was damaged and rotten; this, nevertheless, we were glad to keep for use.

I had hitherto been scarcely able to keep any account of our run; but we now equipped ourselves a little better, by getting a log-line marked, and, having practised at counting seconds, several could do it with some degree of exactness.

At noon I observed, in latitude 18° 10′ S., and considered my course and distance from yesterday noon, N.W. by W. ¼ W., 94 miles; longitude, by account, from Tofoa 4° 29′ W.

For dinner, I served some of the damaged bread, and a quarter of a pint of water.

About six o'clock in the afternoon, we discovered two islands, one bearing W. by S. 6 leagues, and the other N.W. by N. 8 leagues; I kept to windward of the northernmost, and passing it by 10 o'clock, I resumed our course to the N.W. and W.N.W. for the night.

Wednesday, 6th.—The weather was fair and the

wind moderate all day from the E.N.E. At daylight, a number of other islands were in sight from S.S.E. to the W., and round to N.E. by E.; between those in the N.W. I determined to pass. At noon a small sandy island or key, two miles distant from me, bore from E. to S. ½ W. I had passed ten islands, the largest of which I judged to be 6 or 8 leagues in circuit. Much larger lands appeared in the S.W. and N.N.W, between which I directed my course. Latitude observed 17° 17' S.; course since yesterday noon N. 50° W.; distance 84 miles; longitude made, by account, 5° 37' W.

Our allowance for the day was a quarter of a pint of cocoa-nut milk, and the meat, which did not exceed two ounces to each person: it was received very contentedly, but we suffered great drought. I durst not venture to land, as we had no arms, and were less capable of defending ourselves than we were at Tofoa.

To keep an account of the boat's run was rendered difficult, from being constantly wet with the sea breaking over us; but, as we advanced towards the land, the sea became smoother, and I was enabled to form a sketch of the islands. Those we were near, appeared fruitful and hilly, some very mountainous, and all of a good height.

To our great joy we hooked a fish, but we were miserably disappointed by its being lost in trying to get it into the boat.

We continued steering to the N.W., between the islands, which, by the evening, appeared of considerable extent, woody and mountainous. At sun-set, the southernmost bore from S. to S.W. by W. and the northernmost from N. by W. ¼ W. to N.E. ¼ E. At six o'clock we were nearly mid-way between them, and about six leagues distant from each shore, when we fell in with a coral bank, on which we had only four feet water, without the least break on it, or ruffle of the sea to give us warning. I could see that it extended about a mile on each side of us.

I directed the course W. by N. for the night, and served to each person an ounce of the damaged bread, and a quarter of a pint of water, for supper.

As our lodgings were very miserable, and confined for want of room, I endeavoured to remedy the latter defect, by putting ourselves at watch and watch; so that one half always sat up while the other lay down on the boat's bottom, or upon a chest, with nothing to cover us but the heavens. Our limbs were dreadfully cramped, for we could not stretch them out; and the nights were so cold, and we so constantly wet, that, after a few hours sleep, we could scarce move.

Thursday 7th.—At dawn of day, we again discovered land from W.S.W. to W.N.W., and another island N.N.W., the latter a high round lump of but little extent: the southern land that we had passed in the night was still in sight. Being very wet and cold, I served a spoonful of rum and a morsel of bread for breakfast.

The land in the west was distinguished by some extraordinary high rocks, which, as we approached them, assumed a variety of forms. The country appeared to be agreeably interspersed with high and low land, and in some places covered with wood. Off the N.E. part lay some small rocky islands, between which and an island 4 leagues to the N.E., I directed my course; but a lee current

very unexpectedly set us very near to the rocky isles, and we could only get clear of it by rowing, passing close to the reef that surrounded them. At this time we observed two large sailing canoes coming swiftly after us along shore, and, being apprehensive of their intentions, we rowed with some anxiety, fully sensible of our weak and defenceless state. At noon it was calm and the weather cloudy; my latitude is therefore doubtful to 3 or 4 miles. Our course since yesterday noon N.W. by W., distance 79 miles; latitude by account, 16° 29' S., and longitude by account, from Tofoa, 6° 46' W. Being constantly wet, it was with the utmost difficulty I could open a book to write, and I am sensible that what I have done can only serve to point out where these lands are to be found again, and give an idea of their extent.

All the afternoon, we had light winds at N.N.E.: the weather was very rainy, attended with thunder and lightning. Only one of the canoes gained upon us, which by three o'clock in the afternoon was not more than two miles off, when she gave over chase.

If I may judge from the sail of these vessels, they are of a similar construction with those at the Friendly Islands, which, with the nearness of their situation, gives reason to believe that they are the same kind of people. Whether these canoes had any hostile intention against us must remain a doubt: perhaps we might have benefited by an intercourse with them; but in our defenceless situation, to have made the experiment would have been risking too much.

I imagine these to be the islands called Feejee, as their extent, direction, and distance from the Friendly Islands, answers to the description given of them by those islanders. Heavy rain came on at four o'clock, when every person did their utmost to catch some water, and we increased our stock to 34 gallons, besides quenching our thirst for the first time since we had been at sea; but an attendant consequence made us pass the night very miserably, for being extremely wet, and having no dry things to shift or cover us, we experienced cold shiverings scarce to be conceived. Most fortunately for us, the forenoon, Friday, 8th, turned out fair, and we stripped and dried our clothes. The allowance I issued to-day, was an ounce and a half of pork, and a tea-spoonful of rum, half-a-pint of cocoa-nut milk, and an ounce of bread. The rum, though so small in quantity, was of the greatest service. A fishing-line was generally towing from the stern of the boat, but though we saw great numbers of fish, we could never catch one.

At noon, I observed, in latitude 16° 4' S, and found we had made a course, from yesterday noon, N. 62° W., distance 62 miles; longitude, by account, from Tofoa, 7° 42' W.

In the afternoon we cleaned out the boat, and it employed us till sun-set to get everything dry and in order. Hitherto I had issued the allowance by guess, but I now made a pair of scales, with two cocoa-nut shells; and, having accidentally some pistol-balls in the boat, 25 of which weighed one pound, or 16 ounces, I adopted one*, as the proportion of weight that each person should receive of bread at the times I served it. I also amused all hands, with describing the situation of

---

* It weighed 272 grains.

New Guinea and New Holland, and gave them every information in my power, that in case any accident happened to me, those who survived might have some idea of what they were about, and be able to find their way to Timor, which at present they knew nothing of, more than the name, and some not even that. At night, I served a quarter of a pint of water, and half an ounce of bread, for supper.

Saturday, 9th.—In the morning, a quarter of a pint of cocoa-nut milk, and some of the decayed bread, was served for breakfast; and for dinner, I divided the meat of four cocoa-nuts, with the remainder of the rotten bread, which was only eatable by such distressed people.

At noon, I observed the latitude to be 15° 47′ S.; course since yesterday N. 75° W., distance sixty-four miles; longitude made, by account, 8° 45′ W.

In the afternoon I fitted a pair of shrouds for each mast, and contrived a canvas weather cloth round the boat, and raised the quarters about nine inches, by nailing on the seats of the stern sheets, which proved of great benefit to us.

The wind had been moderate all day in the S. E. quarter, with fine weather; but, about nine o'clock in the evening, the clouds began to gather, and we had a prodigious fall of rain, with severe thunder and lightning. By midnight we caught about twenty gallons of water. Being miserably wet and cold, I served to the people a tea-spoonful of rum each, to enable them to bear with their distressed situation. The weather continued extremely bad and the wind increased; we spent a very miserable night, without sleep, except such as could be got in the midst of rain. The day brought no relief but its light. The sea broke over us so much that two men were constantly baling; and we had no choice how to steer, being obliged to keep before the waves for fear of the boat filling.

The allowance now regularly served to each person was one 25th of a pound of bread, and a quarter of a pint of water at eight in the morning, at noon, and at sun-set. To-day I gave about half an ounce of pork for dinner, which, though any moderate person would have considered only as a mouthful, was divided into three or four.

The rain abated towards noon, and I observed the latitude to be 15° 17′ S.; course N. 67° W., distance seventy-eight miles; longitude made 10° W.

The wind continued strong from S. S. E. to S. E., with very squally weather and a high breaking sea, so that we were miserably wet, and suffered great cold in the night.

Monday, 11th.—In the morning at day-break, I served to every person a tea-spoonful of rum, our limbs being so cramped that we could scarce move them. Our situation was now extremely dangerous, the sea frequently running over our stern, which kept us baling with all our strength.

At noon the sun appeared, which gave us as much pleasure as in a winter's day in England. I issued the 25th of a pound of bread, and a quarter of a pint of water as yesterday. Latitude observed 14° 50′ S.; course 71° W., distance 102 miles; and longitude, by account, 11° 39′ W. from Tofoa.

In the evening it rained hard, and we again experienced a dreadful night. At length the day (Tuesday the 12th) came, and showed to me a miserable set of beings, full of wants, without anything to relieve them. Some complained of great pain in their bowels, and every one of having almost lost the use of his limbs. The little sleep we got was no ways refreshing, as we were covered with sea and rain. I served a spoonful of rum at day-dawn, and the usual allowance of bread and water for breakfast, dinner, and supper.

At noon it was almost calm, no sun to be seen, and some of us shivering with cold. Course since yesterday, W. by N., distance eighty-nine miles; latitude, by account, 14° 33′ S.; longitude made 13° 9′ W. The direction of our course was to pass to the northward of the New Hebrides.

The wet weather continued, and in the afternoon the wind came from the southward, blowing fresh in squalls. As there was no prospect of getting our clothes dried, I recommended to every one to strip, and wring them through the salt water, by which means they received a warmth that, while wet with rain, they could not have.

This afternoon we saw a kind of fruit on the water, which Nelson told me was the Barringtonia of Forster; and as I saw the same again in the morning, and some men-of-war birds, I was led to believe that we were not far from land.

We continued constantly shipping seas and baling, and were very wet and cold in the night; but I could not afford the allowance of rum at day-break.

Wednesday, 13th.—At noon I had a sight of the sun, latitude 14° 17′ S.; course W. by N. seventy-nine miles; longitude made 14° 28′ W. All this day we were constantly shipping water, and suffered much cold and shiverings in the night.

Thursday, 14th.—Fresh gales at S. E., and gloomy weather, with rain and a high sea. At six in the morning we saw land, from S. W. by S. eight leagues, to N. W. by W. ¼ W. six leagues, which soon after appeared to be four islands, one of them much larger than the others, and all of them high and remarkable. At noon, we discovered a small island and some rocks, bearing N. W. by N. four leagues, and another island W. eight leagues, so that the whole were six in number; the four I had first seen bearing from S. ¼ E. to S. W. by S.; our distance three leagues from the nearest island. My latitude observed was 13° 29′ S., and longitude by account, from Tofoa, 15° 49′ W.; course, since yesterday noon, N. 63° W., distance eighty-nine miles. At four in the afternoon we passed the westernmost island.

Friday, 15th.—At one in the morning another island was discovered, bearing W. N. W., five leagues distance, and at eight we saw it for the last time, bearing N. E. seven leagues. A number of gannets, boobies, and men-of-war birds were seen.

These islands lie between the latitude of 12° 16′ and 14° 10′ S.; their longitude, according to my reckoning, 15° 51′ to 17° 6′ W. from the island Tofoa *. The largest island I judged to be about

---

* By making a proportional allowance for the error afterwards found in the dead reckoning, I estimate the longitude of these islands to be from 167° 17′ E. to 168° 34′ E. from Greenwich.

twenty leagues in circuit, the others five or six. The easternmost is the smallest island, and most remarkable, having a high sugar-loaf hill.

The sight of these islands served only to increase the misery of our situation. We were very little better than starving, with plenty in view; yet to attempt procuring any relief was attended with so much danger, that prolonging of life, even in the midst of misery, was thought preferable, while there remained hopes of being able to surmount our hardships. For my own part, I consider the general run of cloudy and wet weather to be a blessing of Providence. Hot weather would have caused us to have died with thirst; and probably, being so constantly covered with rain or sea protected us from that dreadful calamity.

As I had nothing to assist my memory, I could not then determine whether these islands were a part of the New Hebrides or not: I believed them to be a new discovery, which I have since found true; but, though they were not seen either by Monsieur Bougainville or Captain Cook, they are so nearly in the neighbourhood of the New Hebrides, that they must be considered as part of the same group. They are fertile and inhabited, as I saw smoke in several places.

The wind was at S. E., with rainy weather all day. The night was very dark, not a star could be seen to steer by, and the sea broke continually over us. I found it necessary to counteract as much as possible the effect of the southerly winds, to prevent being driven too near New Guinea; for in general we were forced to keep so much before the sea, that if we had not at intervals of moderate weather, steered a more southerly course, we should inevitably, from a continuance of the gales, have been thrown in sight of that coast: in which case there would most probably have been an end to our voyage.

Saturday, the 16th.—In addition to our miserable allowance of one 25th of a pound of bread, and a quarter of a pint of water, I issued for dinner about an ounce of salt pork to each person. I was often solicited for this pork, but I considered it more proper to issue it in small quantities than to suffer it to be all used at once or twice, which would have been done if I had allowed it.

At noon I observed, in 13° 33' S.; longitude made from Tofoa, 19° 27' W.; course, N. 82° W., distance 101 miles. The sun breaking out through the clouds, gave us hopes of drying our wet clothes; but the sunshine was of short duration. We had strong breezes at S. E. by S., and dark gloomy weather, with storms of thunder, lightning, and rain. The night was truly horrible, and not a star to be seen, so that our steerage was uncertain.

Sunday, the 17th.—At dawn of day I found every person complaining, and some of them solicited extra allowance, which I positively refused. Our situation was miserable; always wet, and suffering extreme cold in the night, without the least shelter from the weather. Being constantly obliged to bale, to keep the boat from filling, was, perhaps, not to be reckoned an evil, as it gave us exercise.

The little rum we had was of great service: when our nights were particularly distressing, I generally served a tea-spoonful or two to each person; and it was always joyful tidings when they heard of my intentions.

At noon a water-spout was very near on board of us. I issued an ounce of pork, in addition to the allowance of bread and water; but before we began to eat every person stripped, and having wrung their clothes through the sea-water, found much warmth and refreshment. Course since yesterday noon, W. S. W., distance 100 miles; latitude, by account, 14° 11' S., and longitude made 21° 3' W.

The night was dark and dismal; the sea constantly breaking over us, and nothing but the wind and waves to direct our steerage. It was my intention, if possible, to make New Holland, to the southward of Endeavour Straits, being sensible that it was necessary to preserve such a situation as would make a southerly wind a fair one; that we might range along the reefs till an opening should be found into smooth water, and we the sooner be able to pick up some refreshments.

Monday, 18th.—In the morning the rain abated, when we stripped, and wrung our clothes through the sea-water as usual, which refreshed us greatly. Every person complained of violent pain in their bones; I was only surprised that no one was yet laid up. The customary allowance of one 25th of a pound of bread, and a quarter of a pint of water, was served at breakfast, dinner, and supper.

At noon I deduced my situation by account, for we had no glimpse of the sun, to be latitude 14° 52' S.; course, since yesterday noon, W. S. W., 106 miles; longitude made from Tofoa 22° 45' W. Saw many boobies and noddies, a sign of being in the neighbourhood of land. In the night we had very severe lightning, with heavy rain; and were obliged to keep baling without intermission.

Tuesday, 19th.—Very bad weather and constant rain. At noon, latitude, by account, 13° 37' S.; course since yesterday, N. 81° W., distance 100 miles; longitude made 24° 33' W. With the allowance of bread and water, served half an ounce of pork to each person for dinner.

Wednesday, 20th.—Fresh breezes E. N. E., with constant rain; at times a deluge. Always baling.

At dawn of day, some of my people seemed half dead: our appearances were horrible; and I could look no way, but I caught the eye of some one in distress. Extreme hunger was now too evident, but no one suffered from thirst, nor had we much inclination to drink, that desire, perhaps, being satisfied through the skin. The little sleep we got was in the midst of water, and we constantly awoke with severe cramps and pains in our bones. This morning I served about two tea-spoonfuls of rum to each person, and the allowance of bread and water as usual. At noon the sun broke out, and revived every one. I found we were in latitude 14° 49' S.; longitude made 25° 46' W.; course S. 88° W., distance, seventy-five miles.

All the afternoon we were so covered with rain and salt water, that we could scarcely see. We suffered extreme cold, and every one dreaded the approach of night. Sleep, though we longed for it, afforded no comfort: for my own part I almost lived without it. About two o'clock in the morning (Tuesday 21st) we were overwhelmed with a deluge of rain. It fell so heavy that we were afraid it would fill the boat, and were obliged to bale with all our might. At dawn of day I served a larger allowance of rum. Towards noon the rain abated and the sun shone, but we were miserably cold and wet, the sea breaking constantly over us; so that, notwithstanding the heavy rain, we had not been able to add to our stock of fresh water. Latitude, by observation, 14° 29′ S., and longitude made, by account from Tofoa, 27° 25′ W.; course, since yesterday noon, N. 78° W., ninety-nine miles. I now considered myself nearly on a meridian with the east part of New Guinea.

Friday, 22nd.—Strong gales from E.S.E. to S.S.E., a high sea, and dark dismal night.

Our situation this day was extremely calamitous. We were obliged to take the course of the sea, running right before it, and watching with the utmost care, as the least error in the helm would in a moment have been our destruction.

At noon it blew very hard, and the foam of the sea kept running over our stern and quarters; I however got propped up, and made an observation of the latitude, in 14° 17′ S.; course N. 85° W., distance 130 miles; longitude made 29° 38′ W.

The misery we suffered this night exceeded the preceding. The sea flew over us with great force, and kept us baling with horror and anxiety. At dawn of day (Saturday 23rd) I found every one in a most distressed condition, and I began to fear that another such night would put an end to the lives of several, who seemed no longer able to support their sufferings. I served an allowance of two tea-spoonfuls of rum; after drinking which, having wrung our clothes, and taken our breakfast of bread and water, we became a little refreshed.

Towards noon the weather became fair, but with very little abatement of the gale, and the sea remained equally high. With some difficulty I observed the latitude to be 13° 44′ S.; course since yesterday noon N. 74° W., distance 116 miles; longitude made 31° 32′ W. from Tofoa.

The wind moderated in the evening, and the weather looked much better, which rejoiced all hands, so that they ate their scanty allowance with more satisfaction than for some time past. The night also was fair; but being always wet with the sea, we suffered much from the cold.—Sunday, 24th. A fine morning, I had the pleasure to see, produce some cheerful countenances; and, the first time for fifteen days past, we experienced comfort from the warmth of the sun. We stripped, and hung our clothes up to dry, which were by this time become so threadbare, that they would not keep out either wet or cold.

At noon I observed in latitude 13° 33′ S.; longitude, by account, from Tofoa 33° 28′ W.; course N. 84° W., distance 114 miles. With the usual allowance of bread and water for dinner, I served an ounce of pork to each person. This afternoon we had many birds about us which are never seen far from land, such as boobies and noddies.

As the sea began to run fair, and we shipped but little water, I took the opportunity to examine into the state of our bread, and found, that according to the present mode of issuing, there was a sufficient quantity remaining for twenty-nine days' allowance; by which time I hoped we should be able to reach Timor. But as this was very uncertain, and it was possible that, after all, we might be obliged to go to Java, I determined to proportion the allowance so as to make our stock hold out six weeks. I was apprehensive that this would be ill received, and that it would require my utmost resolution to enforce it; for, small as the quantity was which I intended to take away for our future good, yet it might appear to my people like robbing them of life; and some, who were less patient than their companions, I expected would very ill brook it. However on my representing the necessity of guarding against delays that might be occasioned in our voyage by contrary winds, or other causes, and promising to enlarge upon the allowance as we got on, they cheerfully agreed to my proposal. It was accordingly settled, that every person should receive one twenty-fifth of a pound of bread for breakfast, and the same quantity for dinner; so that by omitting the proportion for supper, we had forty-three days' allowance.

Monday, 25th.—At noon some noddies came so near to us, that one of them was caught by hand. This bird was about the size of a small pigeon. I divided it, with its entrails, into eighteen portions, and by a well-known method at sea, of, *Who shall have this*?[*] it was distributed, with the allowance of bread and water for dinner, and eat up bones and all, with salt water for sauce. I observed the latitude 13° 32′ S.; longitude made 35° 19′ W.; course N. 89° W., distance 108 miles.

In the evening, several boobies flying very near to us, we had the good fortune to catch one of them. This bird is as large as a duck: like the noddy, it has received its name from seamen, for suffering itself to be caught on the masts and yards of ships. They are the most presumptive proofs of being in the neighbourhood of land of any sea-fowl we are acquainted with. I directed the bird to be killed for supper, and the blood to be given to three of the people who were the most distressed for want of food. The body, with the entrails, beak, and feet, I divided into eighteen shares, and with an allowance of bread, which I made a merit of granting, we made a good supper, compared with our usual fare.

Tuesday, 26th.—Fresh breezes from the S.E., with fine weather. In the morning we caught another booby, so that Providence appeared to be relieving our wants in an extraordinary manner. Towards noon, we passed a great many pieces of the branches of trees, some of which appeared to have been no long time in the water. I had a good observation for the latitude, and found our situation to be in 13° 41′ S.; longitude, by account, from Tofoa, 37° 13′ W.; course S. 85° W., 112 miles. The people were overjoyed at the addition to their dinner, which was distributed in the same manner as on the preceding evening; giving the blood to those who were the most in want of food.

[*] One person turns his back on the object that is to be divided; another then points separately to the portions, at each of them asking aloud, "Who shall have this?" to which the first answers by naming somebody. This impartial method of division gives every man an equal chance of the best share.

To make the bread a little savoury, most of the people frequently dipped it in salt water; but I generally broke mine into small pieces, and ate it in my allowance of water, out of a cocoa-nut shell, with a spoon; economically avoiding to take too large a piece at a time, so that I was as long at dinner as if it had been a much more plentiful meal.

The weather was now serene, which, nevertheless, was not without its inconveniences, for we began to feel distress of a different kind from that which we had lately been accustomed to suffer. The heat of the sun was so powerful, that several of the people were seized with a languor and faintness, which made life indifferent. We were so fortunate as to catch two boobies in the evening; their stomachs contained several flying-fish and small cuttle-fish, all of which I saved to be divided for dinner the next day.

Wednesday, 27th.—A fresh breeze at E. S. E., with fair weather. We passed much drift-wood this forenoon, and saw many birds; I therefore did not hesitate to pronounce that we were near the reefs of New Holland. From my recollection of Captain Cook's survey of this coast, I considered the direction of it to be N.W., and I was therefore satisfied that, with the wind to the southward of E., I could always clear any dangers.

At noon, I observed in latitude 13° 26′ S.; course since yesterday N. 82° W., distance 109 miles; longitude made 39° 4′ W. After writing my account, I divided the two birds with their entrails, and the contents of their maws, into eighteen portions, and, as the prize was a very valuable one, it was divided as before, by calling out, *Who shall have this?* so that to-day, with the allowance of a twenty-fifth of a pound of bread at breakfast, and another at dinner, with the proportion of water, I was happy to see that every person thought he had feasted.

In the evening, we saw a gannet; and the clouds remained so fixed in the west, that I had little doubt of our being near the land. The people, after taking their allowance of water for supper, amused themselves with conversing on the probability of what we should find.

Thursday, 28th.—At one in the morning, the person at the helm heard the sound of breakers, and I no sooner lifted up my head, than I saw them close under our lee, not more than a quarter of a mile distant from us. I immediately hauled on a wind to the N.N.E., and in ten minutes' time we could neither see nor hear them.

I have already mentioned my reason for making New Holland so far to the southward: for I never doubted of numerous openings in the reef, through which I could have access to the shore: and, knowing the inclination of the coast to be to the N.W., and the wind mostly to the southward of E., I could with ease range such a barrier of reefs till I should find a passage, which now became absolutely necessary, without a moment's loss of time. The idea of getting into smooth water, and finding refreshments, kept my people's spirits up: their joy was very great after we had got clear of the breakers, to which we had approached much nearer than I thought was possible, without first discovering them.

In the morning, at day-light, we could see nothing of the land or of the reefs. We bore away again, and at nine o'clock, saw the reefs. The sea broke furiously over every part, and we had no sooner got near to them, than the wind came at E., so that we could only lie along the line of the breakers; within which we saw the water so smooth, that every person already anticipated the heart-felt satisfaction he should receive, as soon as we could get within them. I now found we were embayed, for we could not lie clear with the sails, the wind having backed against us; and the sea set in so heavy towards the reef, that our situation was become unsafe. We could effect but little with the oars, having scarce strength to pull them; and I began to apprehend that we should be obliged to attempt pushing over the reef. Even this I did not despair of effecting with success, when happily we discovered a break in the reef, about one mile from us, and at the same time an island of a moderate height within it, nearly in the same direction, bearing W. ½ N. I entered the passage with a strong stream running to the westward, and found it about a quarter of a mile broad, with every appearance of deep water.

On the outside, the reef inclined to the N.E. for a few miles, and from thence to the N.W.: on the south side of the entrance, it inclined to the S.S.W. as far as I could see it; and I conjecture that a similar passage to this which we now entered, may be found near the breakers that I first discovered, which are twenty-three miles S. of this channel.

Being now happily within the reefs, and in smooth water, I endeavoured to keep near them to try for fish; but the tide set us to the N.W., I therefore bore away in that direction, and, having promised to land on the first convenient spot we could find, all our past hardships seemed already to be forgotten.

My longitude, made by dead reckoning, from the island Tofoa to our passage through the reef, is 40° 10′ W. Providential Channel, I imagine, must lie very nearly under the same meridian with our passage; by which it appears we had outrun our reckoning 1° 9′.

We now returned God thanks for his gracious protection, and with much content took our miserable allowance of a twenty-fifth of a pound of bread, and a quarter of a pint of water, for dinner.

CHAPTER XVI.

PROGRESS TO THE NORTHWARD, ALONG THE COAST OF NEW HOLLAND—LAND ON DIFFERENT ISLANDS, IN SEARCH OF SUPPLIES.

As we advanced within the reefs, the coast began to show itself very distinctly, in a variety of high and low land; some parts of which were covered with wood. In our way towards the shore, we fell in with a point of a reef which is connected with that towards the sea, and here we came to a grapnel, and tried to catch fish, but had no success. Two islands lay about four miles to the W. by N., and appeared eligible for a resting-place, if for nothing more; but on our approach to the nearest island, it proved to be only a heap of stones, and its size too inconsiderable to shelter the boat. We therefore proceeded to the next, which was close to it and towards the main. On the N.W. side of this, I found a bay and a fine sandy point to land at. Our distance was about a quarter of a mile from a projecting part of the main, which bore from S.W. by S., to N.N.W. ¼ W. We landed to examine if there were any signs of the natives being near us : we saw some old fire-places, but nothing to make me apprehend that this would be an unsafe situation for the night. Every one was anxious to find something to eat, and it was soon discovered that there were oysters on these rocks, for the tide was out ; but it was nearly dark, and only a few could be gathered. I determined therefore to wait till the morning, when I should better know how to proceed, and I directed that one half of our company should sleep on shore, and the other half in the boat. We would gladly have made a fire, but, as we could not accomplish it, we took our rest for the night, which happily was calm and undisturbed.

Friday, 29th.—The dawn of day brought greater strength and spirits to us than I expected ; for, notwithstanding every one was very weak, there appeared strength sufficient remaining to make me conceive the most favourable hopes of our being able to surmount the difficulties we might yet have to encounter.

As there were no appearances to make me imagine that any of the natives were near us, I sent out parties in search of supplies, while others of the people were putting the boat in order, that we might be ready to go to sea in case any unforeseen cause should make it necessary. One of the gud-geons of the rudder had come out in the course of the night, and was lost. This, if it had happened at sea, might have been attended with the most serious consequences, as the management of the boat could not have been so nicely preserved as these very heavy seas required. I had been apprehensive of this accident, and had in some measure prepared for it, by having grummets fixed on each quarter of the boat for oars ; but our utmost readiness in using them, would not probably have saved us. It appears, therefore, a providential circumstance, that it happened in a place of safety, and that it was in our power to remedy the defect ; for by great good luck we found a large staple in the boat, which answered the purpose.

The parties returned, highly rejoiced at having found plenty of oysters and fresh water. I had also made a fire, by the help of a small magnifying glass ; and, what was still more fortunate, we found among the few things which had been thrown into the boat and saved, a piece of brim-stone and a tinder-box, so that I secured fire for the future.

One of the people had been so provident as to bring away with him from the ship, a copper pot : by being in possession of this article we were ena-bled to make a proper use of the supply we now obtained ; for, with a mixture of bread, and a little pork, we made a stew that might have been relished by people of far more delicate appetites, and of which each person received a full pint.

The general complaints of disease among us, were a dizziness in the head, great weakness of the joints, and violent tenesmus ; most of us hav-ing had no evacuation by stool since we left the ship. I had constantly a severe pain at my stomach ; but none of our complaints were alarming : on the contrary, every one retained marks of strength, that, with a mind possessed of a tolerable share of fortitude, seemed able to bear more fatigue than I imagined we should have to undergo in our voyage to Timor.

As I would not allow the people to expose them-selves to the heat of the sun, it being near noon, every one took his allotment of earth where it was shaded by the bushes, for a short sleep.

The oysters which we found, grew so fast to the rocks, that it was with difficulty they could be broken off ; and at length we discovered it to be the most expeditious way to open them where they were fixed. They were of a good size, and well tasted. To add to this happy circumstance, in the hollow of the land there grew some wire-grass, which indicated a moist situation. On forcing a stick, about three feet long, into the ground, we found water, and with little trouble dug a well, which produced as much as our occasions required. It was very good, but I could not determine if it was a spring or not. We were not obliged to make the well deep, for it flowed as fast as we emptied it ; which, as the soil was apparently too loose to retain water from the rains, renders it probable to be a spring. On the south side of the island, like-wise, we found a small run of good water.

Besides places where fires had been made, there were other signs of the natives sometimes resorting to this island. I saw two ill-constructed huts or wigwams, which had only one side loosely covered ; and a pointed stick was found, about three feet long, with a slit in the end of it, to sling stones with ; the same as the natives of Van Die-men's Land use.

The track of some animal was very discernible, and Nelson agreed with me that it was the kan-garoo ; but whether these animals swim over from the main-land, or are brought here by the natives to breed, it is impossible to determine. The latter is not improbable ; as they may be taken with less difficulty in a confined spot like this, than on the continent.

The island is about a league in circuit : it is a high lump of rocks and stones covered with wood ; but the trees are small, the soil, which is very indifferent and sandy, being barely sufficient to produce them. The trees that came within our knowledge were the manchineal and a species of purow : also some palm-trees, the tops of which we cut down, and the soft interior part or heart of them was so palatable that it made a good addi-tion to our mess. Nelson discovered some fern roots, which I thought might be good roasted, as a substitute for bread, but in this I was mistaken ; it however was very serviceable in its natural state to allay thirst, and on that account I directed a quantity to be collected to take into the boat. Many pieces of cocoa-nut shells and husk were found about the shore, but we could find no cocoa-nut trees, neither did I see any on the main.

I had cautioned the people not to touch any kind of berry or fruit that they might find ; yet they were no sooner out of my sight than they began to make free with three different kinds, that grew all over the island, eating without any re-serve. The symptoms of having eaten too much began at last to frighten some of them ; but on questioning others, who had taken a more mode-rate allowance, their minds were a little quieted.

E 2

The others, however, became equally alarmed in their turn, dreading that such symptoms would come on, and that they were all poisoned, so that they regarded each other with the strongest marks of apprehension, uncertain what would be the issue of their imprudence. Fortunately the fruit proved wholesome and good. One sort grew on a small delicate kind of vine; they were the size of a large gooseberry, and very like in substance, but had only a sweet taste: the skin was a pale red, streaked with yellow the long way of the fruit: it was pleasant and agreeable. Another kind grew on bushes, like that which is called the sea-side grape in the West Indies; but the fruit was very different, being more like elder-berries, and grew in clusters in the same manner. The third sort was a blackberry; this was not in such plenty as the others, and resembled a bullace, or large kind of sloe, both in size and taste. When I saw that these fruits were eaten by the birds, I no longer doubted of their being wholesome, and those who had already tried the experiment, not finding any bad effect, made it a certainty that we might eat of them without danger.

Wild pigeons, parrots, and other birds, were about the summit of the island, but, having no fire-arms, relief of that kind was not to be expected, unless we should find some unfrequented spot where the birds were so tame that we might take them with our hands.

The shore of this island is very rocky, except the place at which we landed, and here I picked up many pieces of pumice-stone. On the part of the main nearest to us, were several sandy bays, which at low-water became an extensive rocky flat. The country had rather a barren appearance, except in a few places where it was covered with wood. A remarkable range of rocks lay a few miles to the S.W., and a high peaked hill seemed to terminate the coast towards the sea, with islands to the southward. A high fair cape showed the direction of the coast to the N.W., about seven leagues distant; and two small isles lay three or four leagues to the northward of our present station.

I saw a few bees or wasps, and several lizards; and the blackberry bushes were full of ants' nests, webbed like a spider's, but so close and compact as not to admit the rain. A trunk of a tree, about 50 feet long, lay on the beach; from which I conclude that a heavy sea sets in here, with a northerly wind.

This day being the anniversary of the restoration of king Charles the Second, and the name not being inapplicable to our present situation (for we were restored to fresh life and strength), I named this Restoration Island; for I thought it probable that Captain Cook might not have taken notice of it. The other names which I have presumed to give the different parts of the coast, are meant only to show my route more distinctly.

At noon, I observed the latitude of the island to be 12° 39′ S.; our course having been N. 66 W°., distance 18 miles from yesterday noon. The wind was at E.S.E., with very fine weather.

In the afternoon, I sent parties out again to gather oysters, with which and some of the inner part of the palm top, we made another good stew for supper, each person receiving a full pint and a half; but I refused bread to this meal, for I considered that our wants might yet be very great, and was intent on saving our principal support whenever it was in my power. After supper, we again divided, and those who were on shore slept by a good fire.

Saturday, 30th.—In the morning, I discovered a visible alteration in our company for the better, and I sent them away again to gather oysters. We had now only two pounds of pork left. This article, which I could not keep under lock and key as I did the bread, had been pilfered by some inconsiderate person, but every one denied having any knowledge of this act; I therefore resolved to put it out of their power for the future, by sharing what remained, for our dinner. While the party was out picking up oysters, I got the boat in readiness for sea, and filled all our water vessels, which amounted to nearly 60 gallons.

The party being returned, dinner was soon ready, which was as plentiful a meal as the supper on the preceding evening, and with the pork I gave an allowance of bread. As it was not yet noon, I sent the people once more to gather oysters for a sea store, recommending to them to be as diligent as possible, for that I was determined to sail in the afternoon.

At noon, I again observed the latitude 12° 39′ S.; it was then high-water, the tide had risen three feet, but I could not be certain from whence the flood came. I deduce the time of high-water at full change to be ten minutes past seven in the morning.

Early in the afternoon, the people returned with the few oysters that they had collected, and every thing was put into the boat. I then examined the quantity of bread remaining, and found thirty-eight days' allowance, according to the last mode of issuing a 25th of a pound at breakfast and at dinner.

Fair weather, and moderate breezes at E. S. E. and S.E.

Being ready for sea, I directed every person to attend prayers. At four o'clock we were preparing to embark; when about twenty of the natives appeared, running and hallooing to us, on the opposite shore. They were each armed with a spear or lance, and a short weapon which they carried in their left hand: they made signs for us to come to them. On the top of the hills we saw the heads of many more; whether these were their wives and children, or others who waited for our landing, meaning not to show themselves, lest we might be intimidated, I cannot say; but, as I found we were discovered to be on the coast, I thought it prudent to make the best of our way, for fear of being pursued by canoes; though, from the accounts of Captain Cook, the chance was that there were very few if any of consequence on any part of the coast. I passed these people as near as I could with safety; they were naked, and apparently black, and their hair or wool bushy and short.

I directed my course within two small islands that lie to the north of Restoration Island, passing between them and the main land, towards Fair Cape, with a strong tide in my favour; so that I was abreast of it by eight o'clock. The coast we passed was high and woody. As I could see no land without Fair Cape, I concluded that the coast inclined to the N.W. and W.N.W.: I therefore steered more towards the W.; but by eleven o'clock at night we met with low land, which inclined to the N.E.; and at three o'clock in the morning I found that we were embayed, which obliged us to stand back for a short time to the southward.

Sunday the 31st.—At day-break, I was exceedingly surprised to find the appearance of the country entirely changed, as if in the course of the night we had been transported to another part of the world; for we had now a low sandy coast in view, with very little verdure, or any thing to indicate that it was at all habitable to a human being, except a few patches of small trees or brushwood.

Many small islands were in sight to the N.E., about six miles distant. The E. part of the main bore N. four miles, and Fair Cape S.S.E. five or six leagues. I took the channel between the nearest island and the main-land, which were about one mile apart, leaving all the islands on the starboard side. Some of these were very pretty spots, covered with wood, and well situated for fishing: large shoals of fish were about us, but we could not catch any. In passing this strait we saw another party of Indians, seven in number, running towards us, shouting and making signs for us to land. Some of them waved green branches of the bushes which were near them, as a token of friendship; but some of their other motions were less friendly. A little farther off, we saw a larger party, who likewise came towards us. I therefore determined not to land, though I much wished to have had some intercourse with these people. Nevertheless I laid the boat close to the rocks, and beckoned to them to approach; but none of them would come within two hundred yards of us. They were armed in the same manner as the people we had seen from Restoration Island; they were stark naked, their colour black, with short bushy hair or wool, and in their appearance were similar to them in every respect. An island of a good height bore N. ¼ W., four miles from us, at which I resolved to land, and from thence to take a look at the coast. At this isle we arrived about eight o'clock in the morning. The shore was rocky, but the water was smooth, and we landed without difficulty. I sent two parties out, one to the northward, and the other to the southward, to seek for supplies, and others I ordered to stay by the boat. On this occasion, fatigue and weakness so far got the better of their sense of duty, that some of the people expressed their discontent at having worked harder than their companions, and declared that they would rather be without their dinner than go in search of it. One person, in particular, went so far as to tell me, with a mutinous look, that he was as good a man as myself. It was not possible for me to judge where this might have an end, if not stopped in time; therefore to prevent such disputes in future, I determined either to preserve my command, or die in the attempt: and, seizing a cutlass, I ordered him to take hold of another and defend himself; on which he called out that I was going to kill him, and immediately made concessions. I did not allow this to interfere further with the harmony of the boat's crew, and every thing soon became quiet.

The parties continued collecting what they could find, which were some fine oysters and clams, and a few small dog-fish that were caught in the holes of the rocks. We also found some rain-water in the hollow of the rocks, on the north part of the island, so that of this essential article we were again so fortunate as to obtain a full supply.

After regulating the mode of proceeding, I walked to the highest part of the island, to consider our route for the night. To my surprise, no more of the main-land could be seen here than from below, the northernmost part in sight, which was full of sand-hills, bearing W. by N., about three leagues. Except the isles to the E.S.E. and S., that we had passed, I could only discover a small key N.W. by N. As this was considerably farther from the main than the spot on which we were at present, I judged it would be a more secure resting-place for the night; for here we were liable to an attack, if the Indians had canoes, as they undoubtedly must have observed our landing. My mind being made up on this point, I returned, after taking a particular look at the island we were on, which I found only to produce a few bushes, and some coarse grass; the extent of the whole not being two miles in circuit. On the north side, in a sandy bay, I saw an old canoe, about thirty-three feet long, lying bottom upwards, and half buried in the beach. It was made of three pieces, the bottom entire, to which the sides were sewed in the common way. It had a sharp projecting prow rudely carved, in resemblance of the head of a fish; the extreme breadth was about three feet, and I imagine it was capable of carrying twenty men. The discovery of so large a canoe, confirmed me in the purpose of seeking a more retired place for our night's lodging.

At noon, the parties were all returned, but had found much difficulty in gathering the oysters, from their close adherence to the rocks, and the clams were scarce: I therefore saw, that it would be of little use to remain longer in this place, as we should not be able to collect more than we could eat. I named this Sunday Island: it lies N. by W. ¼ W. from Restoration Island; the latitude, by a good observation, 11° 58′ S.

We had a fresh breeze at S.E. by S., with fair weather. At two o'clock in the afternoon, we dined; each person having a full pint and a half of stewed oysters and clams, thickened with small beans, which Nelson informed me were a species of dolichos. Having eaten heartily, and completed our water, I waited to determine the time of high-water, which I found to be at three o'clock, and the rise of the tide about five feet. According to this, it is high-water on the full and change, at nineteen minutes past nine in the morning: I observed the flood to come from the southward, though, at Restoration Island, I thought it came from the northward. I think Captain Cook mentions that he found great irregularity in the set of the flood on this coast.

We steered for the key seen in the N.W. by N., where we arrived just at dark, but found it so surrounded by a reef of rocks, that I could not land without danger of staving the boat; and on that account we came to a grapnel for the night.

Monday, June the 1st.—At dawn of day, we got on shore, and tracked the boat into shelter; for the wind blowing fresh without, and the ground being rocky, it was not safe to trust her at a grapnel, lest she should be blown to sea: I was, therefore, obliged to let her ground in the course of the ebb. From appearances, I expected that if we remained till night we should meet with turtle, as we discovered recent tracks of them. Innumerable birds of the noddy kind made this island their resting-place; so that we had reason to flatter ourselves with hopes of getting supplies in greater abundance than it had hitherto been in our power. Our situation was at least four leagues distant from the main. We were on the north-westernmost of four small keys, which were surrounded by a reef of rocks connected by sand-banks, except between the two northernmost; and there likewise it was dry at low water; the whole forming a lagoon island, into which the tide flowed: at this entrance I kept the boat.

As usual, I sent parties away in search of supplies, but to our great disappointment, we could only get a few clams and some dolichos: with these, and the oysters we had brought from Sunday Island, I made up a mess for dinner, with the addition of a small quantity of bread.

Towards noon, Nelson, and some others, who had been to the easternmost key, returned; but Nelson was in so weak a condition, that he was obliged to be supported by two men. His complaint was a violent heat in his bowels, a loss of sight, much drought, and an inability to walk. This I found was occasioned by his being unable to support the heat of the sun, and that, when he was fatigued and faint, instead of retiring into the shade to rest, he had continued to attempt more than his strength was equal to. I was glad to find that he had no fever; and it was now that the little wine, which I had so carefully saved, became of real use. I gave it in very small quantities, with some pieces of bread soaked in it; and he soon began to recover. The boatswain and carpenter also were ill, and complained of head-ach, and sickness of the stomach. Others, who had not had any evacuations by stool, became shockingly distressed with the tenesmus; so that there were but few without complaints. An idea prevailed, that the sickness of the boatswain and carpenter was occasioned by eating the dolichos. Myself, however, and some others, who had taken the same food, felt no inconvenience; but the truth was, that many of the people had eaten a large quantity of them raw, and Nelson informed me, that they were constantly teasing him, whenever a berry was found, to know if it was good to eat; so that it would not have been surprising if many of them had been really poisoned.

Our dinner was not so well relished as at Sunday Island, because we had mixed the dolichos with our stew. The oysters and soup, however, were eaten by every one, except Nelson, whom I fed with a few small pieces of bread soaked in half a glass of wine, and he continued to mend.

In my walk round the island, I found several cocoa-nut shells, the remains of an old wigwam, and the backs of two turtle, but no sign of any quadruped. One of the people found three sea-fowl's eggs.

As is common on such spots, the soil is little other than sand, yet it produced small tea-trees, and some others, that we were not acquainted with. There were fish in the lagoon, but we could not catch any. Our wants, therefore, were not likely to be supplied here, not even with water for our daily expense: nevertheless, I determined to wait till the morning, that we might try our success in the night for turtle and birds. A quiet night's rest also, I conceived, would be of essential service to those who were unwell.

The wigwam and turtle shell, were proofs that the natives at times visited this place: and that they had canoes, the remains of the large canoe that we saw at Sunday Island, left no room to doubt: but I did not apprehend that we ran any risk by remaining here a short time. I directed our fire, however, to be made in the thicket, that we might not be discovered by its light.

At noon, I observed the latitude of this island to be 11° 47′ S. The main-land extended towards the N. W., and was full of white sand-hills: another small island lay within us, bearing W. by N. ¼ N., three leagues distant. Our situation being very low, we could see nothing of the reef towards the sea.

The afternoon was advantageously spent in sleep. There were, however, a few not disposed to it, and those were employed in dressing some clams to take with us for the next day's dinner: others we cut up in slices to dry, which I knew was the most valuable supply we could find here; but they were very scarce.

Towards evening, I cautioned every one against making too large a fire, or suffering it after dark to blaze up. Mr. Samuel and Mr. Peckover had the superintendence of this business, while I was strolling about the beach to observe if I thought it could be seen from the main. I was just satisfied that it could not, when on a sudden the island appeared all in a blaze, that might have been discerned at a much more considerable distance. I ran to learn the cause, and found that it was occasioned by the imprudence and obstinacy of one of the party, who, in my absence, had insisted on having a fire to himself; in making which the flames caught the neighbouring grass and rapidly spread. This misconduct might have produced very serious consequences, by discovering our situation to the natives; for, if they had attacked us, we had neither arms nor strength to oppose an enemy. Thus the relief which I expected from a little sleep was totally lost, and I anxiously waited for the flowing of the tide, that we might proceed to sea.

It was high-water at half past five this evening, whence I deduced the time, on the full and change of the moon, to be 58′ past ten in the morning: the rise was nearly five feet. I could not observe the set of the flood; but imagined it to come from the southward, and that I was mistaken at Restoration Island, as I found the time of high-water gradually later the more we advanced to the northward.

At Restoration Island, high-water,		
full and change	7ʰ	10′
Sunday Island	9	19
Here	10	58

After eight o'clock, Mr. Samuel and Mr. Peckover went out to watch for turtle, and three men went to the east key to endeavour to catch birds. All the others complaining of being sick, took their rest, except Mr. Hayward and Mr. Elphinston, whom I directed to keep watch. About midnight the bird party returned, with only twelve noddies, birds which I have already described to be about the size of pigeons : but if it had not been for the folly and obstinacy of one of the party, who separated from the other two, and disturbed the birds, they might have caught a great number. I was so much provoked at my plans being thus defeated, that I gave this offender* a good beating. I now went in search of the turtling party, who had taken great pains, but without success. This did not surprise me, as it was not to be expected that turtle would come near us, after the noise which had been made at the beginning of the evening in extinguishing the fire. I therefore desired them to come back, but they requested to stay a little longer, as they still hoped to find some before daylight : however, they returned by three o'clock, without any reward for their labour.

The birds we half dressed, that they might keep the better : and these, with a few clams, made the whole of the supply procured here. I tied a few gilt buttons and some pieces of iron to a tree, for any of the natives that might come after us ; and, finding my invalids much better for their night's rest, we embarked, and departed by dawn of day. Wind at S.E. ; course to the N. by W.

Tuesday, 2nd.—When we had run two leagues to the northward, the sea suddenly became rough, which not having before experienced since we were within the reefs, I concluded to be occasioned by an open channel to the ocean. Soon afterwards, we met with a large shoal, on which were two sandy keys ; between these and two others, four miles to the west, I passed on to the northward, the sea still continuing to be rough.

Towards noon, I fell in with six other keys, most of which produced some small trees and brush-wood. These formed a pleasing contrast with the main-land we had passed, which was full of sand-hills. The country continued hilly, and the northernmost land, the same we had seen from the lagoon island, appeared like downs, sloping towards the sea. Nearly abreast of us, was a flat-topped hill, which on account of its shape, I called Pudding-pan hill ; and a little to the northward were two other hills, which we called the Paps ; and here was a small tract of country without sand, the eastern part of which forms a cape, whence the coast inclines to the N.W. by N.

I divided six birds, and issued one 25th of a pound of bread, with half a pint of water, to each person for dinner, and I gave half a glass of wine to Nelson, who was now so far recovered as to require no other indulgence.

The gunner, when he left the ship, brought his watch with him, by which we had regulated our time till to-day, when unfortunately it stopped ; so that noon, sun-rise, and sun-set, are the only parts of the twenty-four hours of which from henceforward I can speak with certainty as to time.

The wind blew fresh from the S.S.E. and S.E. all the afternoon, with fair weather. As we stood to the N. by W., we found more sea, which I attributed to our receiving less shelter from the reefs to the eastward : it is probable they do not extend so far north as this ; at least it may be

concluded that there is not a continued barrier to prevent shipping having access to the shore. I observed that the stream set to the N.W., which I considered to be the flood. In some places along the coast we saw patches of wood. At five o'clock, steering to the N.W., we passed a large and fair inlet, into which, I imagine, there is a safe and commodious entrance ; it lies in latitude 11° S. About three leagues to the northward of this is an island at which we arrived about sunset, and took shelter for the night under a sandy point, which was the only part we could land at. This being rather a wild situation, I thought it best to sleep in the boat : nevertheless I sent a party away to see if any thing could be got, but they returned without success. They saw a great number of turtle bones and shells, where the natives had been feasting, and their last visit seemed to be of late date. The island was covered with wood, but in other respects it was a lump of rocks.

Wednesday, 3rd.—We lay at a grapnel till daylight, with a very fresh gale and cloudy weather. We continued steering to the N.W. Several islands and keys were in sight to the northward : the most northerly island was mountainous, having on it a very high round hill ; and a smaller was remarkable for a single peaked hill. I was now tolerably certain that we should be clear of New Holland in the afternoon.

As an addition to our dinner of bread and water, I served to each person six oysters.

At two o'clock in the afternoon, as we were steering to the S.W., towards the westernmost part of the land in sight, we fell in with some large sand-banks that run off from the coast : I therefore called this Shoal Cape. We were obliged to steer to the northward again, till we got round the shoals, when I directed the course to the W.

At four o'clock, the westernmost of the islands to the northward bore N. four leagues : Wednesday Island E. by N. five leagues ; and Shoal Cape S.E. by E. two leagues. A small island was seen bearing W., at which we arrived before dark, and found that it was only a rock where boobies resort, for which reason I called it Booby Island. Here terminated the rocks and shoals of the N. part of New Holland, for, except Booby Island, no land was seen to the westward of S., after three o'clock this afternoon.

CHAPTER XVII.

PASSAGE FROM NEW HOLLAND TO THE ISLAND TIMOR—ARRIVE AT COUPANG—RECEPTION THERE.

On Wednesday, June 3rd, at eight o'clock in the evening, we once more launched into the open ocean. Miserable as our situation was in every respect, I was secretly surprised to see that it did not appear to affect any one so strongly as myself ; on the contrary, it seemed as if they had embarked on a voyage to Timor in a vessel sufficiently calculated for safety and convenience. So much confidence gave me great pleasure, and I may venture to assert, that to this cause our preservation is chiefly to be attributed.

I encouraged every one with hopes that eight or ten days would bring us to a land of safety ; and, after praying to God for a continuance of

---

* Robert Lamb.—This man, when he came to Java, acknowledged he had eaten nine birds raw, after he separated from his two companions.

his most gracious protection, I served an allowance of water for supper, and directed our course to the W.S.W., to counteract the southerly winds, in case they should blow strong.

We had been just six days on the coast of New Holland, in the course of which we found oysters, a few clams, some birds, and water. But perhaps a benefit nearly equal to this we received, by having been relieved from the fatigue of being constantly in the boat, and enjoying good rest at night. These advantages certainly preserved our lives; and small as the supply was, I am very sensible how much it alleviated our distresses. By this time nature must have sank under the extremes of hunger and fatigue. Some would have ceased to struggle for a life that only promised wretchedness and misery; and others, though possessed of more bodily strength, must soon have followed their unfortunate companions. Even in our present situation, we were most deplorable objects; but the hopes of a speedy relief kept up our spirits. For my own part, incredible as it may appear, I felt neither extreme hunger nor thirst. My allowance contented me, knowing that I could have no more.

Thursday, 4th.—I served one 25th of a pound of bread, and an allowance of water for breakfast, and the same for dinner, with an addition of six oysters to each person. At noon, latitude observed 10° 48' S.; course since yesterday noon, S. 81° W., distance 111 miles; longitude, by account, from Shoal Cape, 1° 45' W. A strong trade wind at E.S.E., with fair weather.

This day we saw a number of water-snakes, that were ringed yellow and black, and towards noon we passed a great deal of rock-weed. Though the weather was fair, we were constantly shipping water, which kept two men always employed to bale the boat.

Friday, 5th.—At noon I observed in latitude 10° 45' S.; our course since yesterday W. ¼ N., 108 miles; longitude made 3° 35' W. Six oysters were as yesterday served to each man, in addition to the usual allowance of bread and water.

In the evening a few boobies came about us, one of which I caught with my hand. The blood was divided among three of the men who were weakest, but the bird I ordered to be kept for our dinner the next day. Served a quarter of a pint of water for supper, and to some, who were most in need, half a pint. In the course of the night, being constantly wet with the sea, we suffered much cold and shiverings.

Saturday, 6th.—At day-light I found that some of the clams, which had been hung up to dry for sea-store, were stolen; but every one solemnly denied having any knowledge of it. This forenoon we saw a gannet, a sand-lark, and some water-snakes, which in general were from two to three feet long.

The usual allowance of bread and water was served for breakfast, and the same for dinner, with the bird, which I distributed in the usual way, of *Who shall have this?* I proposed to make Timor about the latitude of 9° 30' S., or 10° S. At noon I observed the latitude to be 10° 19' S.; course N. 77° W., distance, 117 miles; longitude made from the Shoal Cape, the north part of New Holland, 5° 31' W.

In the afternoon I took an opportunity of examining our store of bread, and found remaining nineteen days' allowance, at the former rate of serving one 25th of a pound three times a day: therefore, as I saw every prospect of a quick passage, I again ventured to grant an allowance for supper, agreeable to my promise at the time it was discontinued.

We passed the night miserably wet and cold, and in the morning I heard heavy complaints. The sea was high and breaking over us. I could only afford the allowance of bread and water for breakfast; but for dinner I gave out an ounce of dried clams to each person, which was all that remained.

At noon I altered the course to the W.N.W., to keep more from the sea, as the wind blew strong. Latitude observed 9° 31' S.; course N. 57° W., distance, eighty-eight miles; longitude made 6° 46' W.

The sea ran very high all this day, and we had frequent showers of rain, so that we were continually wet, and suffered much cold in the night. Mr. Ledward, the surgeon, and Lawrence Lebogue, an old hardy seaman, appeared to be giving way very fast. I could only assist them by a teaspoonful or two of wine, which I had carefully saved, expecting such a melancholy necessity.

Monday, 8th.—Wind at S.E. The weather was more moderate than it had been for some days past. A few gannets were seen. At noon I observed 9° 45' S.; course W.N.W. ¼ W., 106 miles; longitude made 8° 23' W. The sea being smooth, I steered W. by S.

At four in the afternoon we caught a small dolphin, which was the first relief of the kind that we obtained. I issued about two ounces to each person, including the offals, and saved the remainder for dinner the next day. Towards evening the wind freshened, and it blew strong all night, so that we shipped much water and suffered greatly from the wet and cold.

Tuesday, 9th.—At day-light as usual I heard much complaining, which my own feelings convinced me was too well founded. I gave the surgeon and Lebogue a little wine, but I could afford them no farther relief, except encouraging them with hopes that a very few days longer, at our present fine rate of sailing, would bring us to Timor.

Gannets, boobies, men of war and tropic birds, were constantly about us. Served the usual allowance of bread and water, and at noon we dined on the remains of the dolphin, which amounted to about an ounce per man. I observed the latitude to be 9° 9' S.; longitude made 10° 8' W.; course, since yesterday noon, S. 76° W.; distance 107 miles.

This afternoon I suffered great sickness from the nature of part of the stomach of the fish, which had fallen to my share at dinner. At sunset I served an allowance of bread and water for supper.

Wednesday, 10th.—In the morning, after a very comfortless night, there was a visible alteration for the worse in many of the people; which gave me great apprehensions. An extreme weakness, swelled legs, hollow and ghastly countenances, a more than common inclination to sleep, with an apparent debility of understanding, seemed to me the melancholy presages of an approaching dissolution. The surgeon and Lebogue in particular, were most miserable objects. I occasionally gave them a few tea-spoonfuls of wine, out of the little that remained, which greatly assisted them. The hopes of being able to accomplish the voyage was our principal support. The boatswain very innocently told me, that he really thought I looked worse than any one in the boat. The simplicity with which he uttered such an opinion amused me, and I returned him a better compliment.

Our latitude at noon, was 9° 16′ S. Longitude from the north part of New Holland, 12° 1′ W. Course since yesterday noon, W. ½ S., 111 miles. Birds and rock-weed showed that we were not far from land; but I expected such signs here, as there are many islands between the east part of Timor and New Guinea. The night was more moderate than the last.

Thursday, 11th. Every one received the customary allowance of bread and water, and an extra allowance of water was given to those who were most in need. At noon I observed in latitude 9° 41′ S.; course S. 77° W., distance 109 miles; longitude made 13° 49′ W. I had little doubt of having now passed the meridian of the eastern part of Timor, which is laid down in 128° E. This diffused universal joy and satisfaction.

In the afternoon, we saw gannets, and many other birds, and at sunset we kept a very anxious look-out. In the evening we caught a booby, which I reserved for our dinner the next day.

Friday, 12th.—At three in the morning, with an excess of joy, we discovered Timor bearing from W.S.W. to W.N.W., and I hauled on a wind to the N.N.E. till day-light, when the land bore from S.W. by S. to N.E. by N. Our distance from the shore, two leagues.

It is not possible for me to describe the pleasure which the blessing of the sight of this land diffused among us. It appeared scarce credible to ourselves, that in an open boat, and so poorly provided, we should have been able to reach the coast of Timor in forty-one days after leaving Tofoa, having in that time run, by our log, a distance of 3618 miles; and that, notwithstanding our extreme distress, no one should have perished in the voyage.

I have already mentioned, that I knew not where the Dutch settlement was situated; but I had a faint idea that it was at the S.W. part of the island. I therefore, after day-light, bore away along shore to the S.S.W., which I was the more readily induced to do, as the wind would not suffer us to go towards the N.E. without great loss of time.

The day gave us a most agreeable prospect of the land, which was interspersed with woods and lawns; the interior part mountainous, but the shore low. Towards noon, the coast became higher, with some remarkable head-lands. We were greatly delighted with the general look of the country, which exhibited many cultivated spots and beautiful situations; but we could only see a few small huts, whence I concluded that no European resided in this part of the island. Much sea ran on the shore, which made landing impracticable. At noon, we were abreast of a high head-land; the extremes of the land bore S.W. ¼ W., and N.N.E. ¼ E.; our distance off shore being three miles; latitude, by observation, 9° 59′ S.; and my longitude, by dead reckoning from the north part of New Holland, 15° 6′ W.

With the usual allowance of bread and water for dinner, I divided the bird we had caught the night before, and to the surgeon and Lebogue I gave a little wine.

The wind blew fresh at E. and E.S.E., with very hazy weather. During the afternoon, we continued our course along a low shore, covered with innumerable palm-trees, called the fan palm, from the leaf spreading like a fan; but here we saw no signs of cultivation, nor had the country so fine an appearance as to the eastward. This, however, was only a small tract, for by sunset it improved again, and I saw several great smokes where the inhabitants were clearing and cultivating their grounds. We had now run twenty-five miles to the W.S.W. since noon, and were W. five miles from a low point, which, in the afternoon, I imagined had been the southernmost land; and here the coast formed a deep bend, with low land in the bight that appeared like islands. The west shore was high; but from this part of the coast to the high cape which we were abreast of at noon, the shore is low, and I believe shoal. I particularly remark this situation, because here the very high ridge of mountains, that run from the east end of the island, terminate, and the appearance of the country changes for the worse.

That we might not run past any settlement in the night, I determined to preserve my station till the morning, and therefore brought to under a close-reefed foresail. We were here in shoal water, our distance from the shore being half a league, the westernmost land in sight bearing W.S.W. ½ W. Served bread and water for supper, and the boat lying to very well, all but the officer of the watch endeavoured to get a little sleep.

Saturday, 13th.—At two in the morning, we wore, and stood in shore till day-light, when I found we had drifted, during the night, about three leagues to the W.S.W., the southernmost land in sight bearing W. On examining the coast, and not seeing any sign of a settlement, we bore away to the westward, having a strong gale, against a weather current, which occasioned much sea. The shore was high and covered with wood; but we did not run far, before low land again formed the coast, the points of which opening at west, I once more fancied we were on the south part of the island; but at ten o'clock we found the coast again inclining towards the south, part of it bearing W.S.W. ½ W. At the same time, high land appeared in the S.W.; but the weather was so hazy, that it was doubtful whether the two lands were separated, the opening only extending one point of the compass. For this reason I stood towards the outer land, and found it to be the island Roti.

I returned to the shore we had left, and brought to a grapnel in a sandy bay, that I might more conveniently calculate my situation. In this place, we saw several smokes, where the natives were clearing their grounds. During the little time we remained here, the master and carpenter very much importuned me to let them go in search of supplies; to which, at length, I assented; but, not finding any other person willing to be of their party, they did not choose to quit the boat. I stopped here no longer than for the purpose just mentioned, and we continued steering along shore. We had a view of a beautiful-looking country, as if formed by art into lawns and parks. The coast is low, and covered with woods, in which are innumerable fan palm-trees, that look like cocoa-nut walks. The interior part is high land, but very different from the more eastern parts of the island, where it is exceedingly mountainous, and, to appearance, the soil better.

At noon, the island Roti bore S.W. by W. seven leagues. I had no observation for the latitude, but by account, we were in 10° 12' S.; our course since yesterday noon being S. 77° W., 54 miles. The usual allowance of bread and water was served for breakfast and dinner, and to the surgeon and Lebogue, I continued to give wine.

We had a strong breeze at E.S.E., with hazy weather, all the afternoon. At two o'clock, having run through a very dangerous breaking sea, the cause of which I attributed to be a strong tide setting to windward, and shoal water, we discovered a spacious bay or sound, with a fair entrance about two or three miles wide. I now conceived hopes that our voyage was nearly at an end, as no place could appear more eligible for shipping, or more likely to be chosen for an European settlement: I therefore came to a grapnel near the east side of the entrance, in a small sandy bay, where we saw a hut, a dog, and some cattle; and I immediately sent the boatswain and gunner away to the hut, to discover the inhabitants.

I had just time to make some nautical obser-vations, when I saw the boatswain and gunner returning with some of the natives: I therefore no longer doubted of our success, and that our expectations would be fully gratified. They brought five Indians, and informed me that they had found two families, where the women treated them with European politeness. From these people I learned, that the governor resided at a place called Cou-pang, which was some distance to the N.E. I made signs for one of them to go in the boat, and show us the way to Coupang, intimating that I would pay him for his trouble: the man readily complied, and came into the boat.

These people were of a dark tawny colour, had long black hair, and chewed a great deal of betel. Their dress was, a square piece of cloth round the hips, in the folds of which was stuck a large knife; a handkerchief wrapped round the head; and another hanging by the four corners from the shoulders, which served as a bag for their betel equipage. They brought us a few pieces of dried turtle, and some ears of Indian corn. This last was the most welcome; for the turtle was so hard, that it could not be eaten without being first soaked in hot water. They offered to bring us some other refreshments if I would wait; but, as the pilot was willing, I determined to push on. It was about half an hour past four when we sailed.

By direction of the pilot, we kept close to the east shore under all our sail; but as night came on, the wind died away, and we were obliged to try at the oars, which I was surprised to see we could use with some effect. At ten o'clock, find-ing we advanced but slowly, I came to a grapnel, and for the first time, I issued double allowance of bread and a little wine to each person.

Sunday, 14th.—At one o'clock in the morning, after the most happy and sweet sleep that ever men enjoyed, we weighed, and continued to keep the east shore on board, in very smooth water; when at last I found we were again open to the sea; the whole of the land to the westward, that we had passed, being an island, which the pilot called Pulo Samow. The northern entrance of this channel is about a mile and a half or two miles wide, and I had no ground at ten fathoms.

The report of two cannon that were fired, gave new life to every one; and soon after we disco-vered two square-rigged vessels and a cutter at anchor to the eastward. We endeavoured to work to windward, but were obliged to take to our oars again, having lost ground on each tack. We kept close to the shore, and continued rowing till four o'clock, when I brought to a grapnel, and gave another allowance of bread and wine to all hands. As soon as we had rested a little, we weighed again, and rowed till near day-light, when we came to a grapnel, off a small fort and town, which the pilot told me was Coupang.

Among the things which the boatswain had thrown into the boat before we left the ship, was a bundle of signal-flags that had been used by the boats to show the depth of water in sounding: with these we had, in the course of the passage, made a small jack, which I now hoisted in the main shrouds, as a signal of distress; for I did not think proper to land without leave.

Soon after day-break, a soldier hailed us to land, which I immediately did, among a crowd of Indians, and was agreeably surprised to meet with an English sailor, who belonged to one of the vessels in the road. His captain, he told me, was the second person in the town; I therefore desired to be conducted to him, as I was informed the governor was ill, and could not then be spoken with.

Captain Spikerman received me with great humanity. I informed him of our distressed situation; and requested that care might be taken of those who were with me, without delay. On which he gave directions for their immediate re-ception at his own house, and went himself to the governor, to know at what time I could be per-mitted to see him; which was fixed to be at eleven o'clock.

I now desired my people to come on shore, which was as much as some of them could do, being scarce able to walk; they, however, were helped to the house, and found tea with bread and butter provided for their breakfast.

The abilities of a painter, perhaps, could seldom have been displayed to more advantage, than in the delineation of the two groups of figures, which at this time presented themselves to each other. An indifferent spectator would have been at a loss which most to admire; the eyes of famine sparkling at immediate relief, or the horror of their preservers at the sight of so many spectres, whose ghastly countenances, if the cause had been unknown, would rather have excited terror than pity. Our bodies were nothing but skin and bones, our limbs were full of sores, and we were clothed in rags: in this condition, with the tears of joy and gratitude flowing down our cheeks, the people of Timor beheld us with a mixture of horror, surprise, and pity.

The governor, Mr. William Adrian Van Este,

notwithstanding extreme ill-health, became so anxious about us, that I saw him before the appointed time. He received me with great affection, and gave me the fullest proofs that he was possessed of every feeling of a humane and good man. Sorry as he was, he said, that such a calamity could ever have happened to us, yet he considered it as the greatest blessing of his life that we had fallen under his protection; and, though his infirmity was so great that he could not do the office of a friend himself, he would give such orders as I might be certain would procure us every supply we wanted. A house should be immediately prepared for me, and, with respect to my people, he said, that I might have room for them either at the hospital or on board of Captain Spikerman's ship, which lay in the road; and he expressed much uneasiness that Coupang could not afford them better accommodations, the house assigned to me being the only one uninhabited, and the situation of the few families that lived at this place such, that they could not conveniently receive strangers. For the present, till matters could be properly regulated, he gave directions that victuals for my people should be dressed at his own house.

On returning to Captain Spikerman's house, I found that every kind relief had been given to my people. The surgeon had dressed their sores, and the cleaning of their persons had not been less attended to, several friendly gifts of apparel having been presented to them.

I desired to be shown to the house that was intended for me, which I found ready, with servants to attend. It consisted of a hall, with a room at each end, and a loft over-head, and was surrounded by a piazza, with an outer apartment in one corner, and a communication from the back part of the house to the street. I therefore determined, instead of separating from my people, to lodge them all with me; and I divided the house as follows: One room I took to myself, the other I allotted to the master, surgeon, Mr. Nelson, and the gunner; the loft to the other officers; and the outer apartment to the men. The hall was common to the officers, and the men had the back piazza. Of this disposition I informed the governor, and he sent down chairs, tables, and benches, with bedding and other necessaries, for the use of every one.

The governor, when I took my leave, had desired me to acquaint him with every thing of which I stood in need; but it was only at particular times that he had a few moments of ease, or could attend to any thing; being in a dying state, with an incurable disease. On this account I transacted whatever business I had, with Mr. Timotheus Wanjon, the second of this place, who was the governor's son-in-law; and who also contributed every thing in his power to make our situation comfortable. I had been, therefore, misinformed by the seaman, who told me that Captain Spikerman was the next person in command to the governor.

At noon, a dinner was brought to the house, sufficiently good to make persons, more accustomed to plenty, eat too much. Yet I believe, few in such a situation would have observed more moderation than my people did. My greatest apprehension was, that they would eat too much

fruit, of which there was great variety in season at this time.

Having seen every one enjoy this meal of plenty, I dined myself with Mr. Wanjon; but I felt no extraordinary inclination to eat or drink. Rest and quiet, I considered as more necessary to the re-establishment of my health, and therefore retired soon to my room, which I found furnished with every convenience. But instead of rest, my mind was disposed to reflect on our late sufferings, and on the failure of the expedition; but above all, on the thanks due to Almighty God, who had given us power to support and bear such heavy calamities, and had enabled me, at last, to be the means of saving eighteen lives.

In times of difficulty, there will generally arise circumstances that bear particularly hard on a commander. In our late situation, it was not the least of my distresses, to be constantly assailed with the melancholy demands of my people for an increase of allowance, which it grieved me to refuse. The necessity of observing the most rigid economy in the distribution of our provisions, was so evident, that I resisted their solicitations, and never deviated from the agreement we made at setting out. The consequence of this care was, that at our arrival we had still remaining sufficient for eleven days, at our scanty allowance: and if we had been so unfortunate as to have missed the Dutch settlement at Timor, we could have proceeded to Java, where I was certain that every supply we wanted could be procured.

Another disagreeable circumstance to which my situation exposed me, was the caprice of ignorant people. Had I been incapable of acting, they would have carried the boat on shore, as soon as we made the island of Timor, without considering that landing among the natives, at a distance from the European settlement, might have been as dangerous as among any other Indians.

The quantity of provisions with which we left the ship, was not more than we should have consumed in five days, had there been no necessity for husbanding our stock. The mutineers must naturally have concluded, that we could have no other place of refuge than the Friendly Islands; for it was not likely they should imagine that, so poorly equipped as we were in every respect, there could have been a possibility of our attempting to return homewards; much less can they suspect that the account of their villany has already reached their native country.

When I reflect how providentially our lives were saved at Tofoa, by the Indians delaying their attack; and that, with scarce any thing to support life, we crossed a sea of more than 1200 leagues, without shelter from the inclemency of the weather; when I reflect that in an open boat, with so much stormy weather, we escaped foundering, that not any of us were taken off by disease, that we had the great good fortune to pass the unfriendly natives of other countries without accident, and at last happily to meet with the most friendly and best of people to relieve our distresses; I say, when I reflect on all these wonderful escapes, the remembrance of such great mercies enables me to bear, with resignation and cheerfulness, the failure of an expedition, the success of which I had so much at heart, and which was frustrated at a time when I was congratulating myself on the fairest prospect of being able to complete it in a manner that would fully have answered the intention of his Majesty, and the humane promoters of so benevolent a plan.

With respect to the preservation of our health, during a course of sixteen days of heavy and almost continual rain, I would recommend to every one in a similar situation, the method we practised, which is, to dip their clothes in the salt water, and wring them out, as often as they become filled with rain :* it was the only resource we had, and I believe was of the greatest service to us, for it felt more like a change of dry clothes than could well be imagined. We had occasion to do this so often, that at length all our clothes were wrung to pieces : for except the few days we passed on the coast of New Holland, we were continually wet either with rain or sea.

Thus, through the assistance of Divine Providence, we surmounted the difficulties and distresses of a most perilous voyage, and arrived safe in an hospitable port, where every necessary and comfort were administered to us with a most liberal hand.

CHAPTER XVIII.

AT COUPANG.

July.—FROM the great humanity and attention of the governor, and the gentlemen at Coupang, we received every kind of assistance, and were not long without evident signs of returning health. Shortly after our arrival, I presented to the governor, a formal account of the loss of the Bounty ; and a requisition, in his Majesty's name, that instructions might be sent to all the Dutch settlements, to stop the ship if she made her appearance. With this a complete descriptive list of the mutineers was given.

I likewise requested, in one of my first visits to the governor, that Nelson might have permission to walk about the country in search of plants, which was readily granted, with an offer of whatever assistance I should think necessary : and the governor assured me that the country was well worth examination, as it abounded with many curious and medicinal plants. From this indulgence I derived no benefit ; for Nelson, who since we left New Holland, had been but in a weak condition, about this time was taken ill, in consequence of a cold caused by imprudently leaving off warm clothing.

To secure our arrival at Batavia, before the October fleet sailed for Europe, I gave public notice of my intention to hire a vessel to carry us to Batavia. In consequence of this notice, several offers were made, but none that I thought reasonable ; which determined me to purchase a small schooner in the road, that was thirty-four feet long ; for which I gave 1000 rix-dollars, and fitted

* The surgeon of the Pandora (the vessel sent to take the mutineers, and which was wrecked on the homeward voyage), makes this observation on the practice here recommended by Captain Bligh : " This is not advisable, if protracted beyond three or four days, as after that time the great absorption from the skin that takes place taints the fluids with the bitter parts of salt water, so that the saliva becomes intolerable in the mouth." The great rains that fell nearly all the time of Captain Bligh's exposure, probably prevented the effects experienced by the crew of the Pandora.

her for sea, under the name of His Majesty's schooner Resource. As the coast of Java is frequently infested with small piratical vessels, it was necessary that we should be provided with the proper means of defence. In this I was assisted by the friendship of Mr. Wanjon, who supplied me with four brass swivels, fourteen stand of small arms and ammunition, which he obligingly let me have as a loan, to be returned at Batavia.

On the 20th of July, I had the misfortune to lose Mr. David Nelson ; he died of an inflammatory fever. The loss of this honest man I very much lamented ; he had, with great care and diligence, attended to the object for which he was sent, and had always been ready to forward every plan that was proposed, for the good of the service in which we were engaged. He was not less useful in our voyage hither, in the course of which he gave me great satisfaction, by the patience and fortitude with which he conducted himself.

July 21st.—This day, I was employed attending the funeral of Mr. Nelson. The corpse was carried by twelve soldiers drest in black, preceded by the minister ; next followed myself and the second governor ; then ten gentlemen of the town and the officers of the ships in the harbour ; and after them my own officers and people.

After reading our burial-service, the body was interred behind the chapel, in the burying-ground appropriated for the Europeans of the town. I was sorry I could get no tombstone to place over his remains.

This was the second voyage Mr. Nelson had undertaken to the South Seas, having been sent out by Sir Joseph Banks, to collect plants, seeds, &c. in Captain Cook's last voyage. And now, after surmounting so many difficulties, and in the midst of thankfulness for his deliverance, he was called upon to pay the debt of nature, at a time least expected.

Our schooner being victualled and ready for sea, on the 20th of August, I took an affectionate leave of the hospitable and friendly inhabitants of Coupang and embarked. In the afternoon we sailed, having the launch, which had so much contributed to our preservation, in tow. We exchanged salutes with the fort and shipping as we ran out of the harbour.

This settlement was formed in the year 1630, and is the only one the Dutch have on the island Timor. They have residents in different parts of the country. On the north side of Timor, there is a Portuguese settlement. The produce of the island is chiefly sandal-wood and bees-wax ; the former article is now scarce. Wax they have in great plenty. The bees build their nests in bushes and in the boughs of trees, to which the natives cannot approach but with fire. The honey is put into jars, and the wax is run into blocks of three feet in length, and from twelve to fifteen inches square. The natives, at least those who live in the neighbourhood of Coupang, are of a very indolent disposition, of which the Chinese have taken advantage ; for though the Malays are very fond of traffic, most of their trade is carried on in small Chinese vessels, of from ten to thirty tons burthen. There is a market at Coupang for the country people, in which, however, there is little business done. I have seen a man from the country, come to market with two potatoes ; and this is not unusual. These being sold for two doits (equal to a halfpenny English) serve to supply him with betel to chew; and the remainder of the day is passed in lounging about the town. The inland people, who live at a distance from the Europeans, are strong and active; but their want of cleanliness, subjects them to filthy diseases.

The chief of the natives, or king of the island, is by the Dutch styled Keyser (emperor). This prince lives at a place called Backennassy, about four miles distant from Coupang. His authority over the natives is not wholly undisputed; which is by the Dutch attributed to the intrigues of the Portuguese, who are on the north part of Timor. The island has lately suffered much by a competition between the present king and one of his nephews, which caused a civil war, that lasted from the beginning of the year 5786 to 1768, when their differences were settled by a treaty chiefly in favour of the king. The ravages committed in these disputes, have occasioned a scarcity of provisions, that probably, from the want of industry in the natives, will not soon be remedied. I had an opportunity of making a visit to the king. His dwelling was a large house, which was divided into only three apartments, and surrounded by a piazza; agreeably situated, but very dirty, as was all the furniture. The king who is an elderly man, received me with much civility, and ordered refreshments to be set before me, which were, tea, rice, cakes, roasted Indian corn, and dried buffalo flesh, with about a pint of arrack; which I believe was all he had. His dress was a cheque wrapper girdled round his waist with a silk and gold belt, a loose linen jacket, and a coarse handkerchief about his head. A few of his chiefs were with him, who partook of our repast; after which the king retired with three of them for a short time, and when he returned, presented me with a round plate of metal about four inches diameter, on which was stamped the figure of a star. As I had been informed that arrack would be an acceptable present, I was prepared to make a return, which was well received. They never dilute their liquor, and, from habit, are able to drink a large quantity of spirits at a time, without being intoxicated.

When a king dies, a large feast is made, to which all the inhabitants are invited. The body, after a few days, is put into a coffin, which is closed up and kept three years before it is interred.

The Dutch have been at some pains to establish Christianity among the natives; but it has not gained much ground, except in the neighbourhood of Coupang. The present king was christened by the name of Barnardus. His Indian name is *Bacchee Bannock*. The Scriptures are translated into the Malay language, and prayers are performed, in the church at Coupang, by a Malay clergyman, in that language.

I met, at Timor, with most of the fruits that are described in Captain Cook's first voyage as natives of Batavia, except the mangostan. The bread-fruit tree, called by the Malays *soccoom*, likewise grows here with great luxuriance, and appears to be as much a native of this island as it is of Otaheite. The fruit is exactly of the same kind, but not so good. A bread-fruit of Timor, weighs half as much more as one of equal size at Otaheite. It is not used here as bread, but generally eaten with milk and sugar. At Backennassy I saw about twenty of the trees, larger than any I have seen at Otaheite. Here is also a sort of bread-fruit tree, that produces seeds, not unlike Windsor beans, and equally palatable, either boiled or roasted. No other part of the fruit is eatable; and though the tree, I am told, is to all appearance the same as the other, the fruits have but little resemblance; the fruit of this being covered with projecting points, nearly half an inch in length.

I received a present of some fine plants, from the governor, which I was afterwards unfortunately obliged to leave at Batavia, for want of proper room to take care of them, in the packet by which I returned to Europe. Mr. Wanjon likewise favoured me with some seeds for his Majesty's garden at Kew, which I had the good fortune to deliver safe, on my return: and some of the mountain rice, cultivated at Timor, on the dry land, which was forwarded to his Majesty's botanic garden at St. Vincent, and to other parts in the West Indies.

A resemblance of language between the people of the South Sea islands, and the inhabitants of many of the islands in the East Indies, has been remarked in Captain Cook's first voyage. Here, the resemblance appeared stronger than has yet been noticed; particularly in their numerals. But besides the language, I observed some customs among the people of Timor, still more striking for their similarity. They practise the *Toogetooge** of the Friendly Islands, which they call *Toombock;* and the *Roomee* of Otaheite, which they call *Ramas*. I likewise saw, placed on their graves, offerings of baskets with tobacco and betel.

I left the governor, Mr. Van Este, at the point of death. To this gentleman our most grateful thanks are due, for the humane and friendly treatment that we received from him. His ill state of health only prevented him from showing us more particular marks of attention. Unhappily, it is to his memory only that I now pay this tribute. It was a fortunate circumstance for us, that Mr. Wanjon, the next in place to the governor, was equally humane and ready to relieve us. His attention was unremitting, and, when there was a doubt about supplying me with money, to enable me to purchase a vessel, he cheerfully took it upon himself; without which, it was evident, I should have been too late at Batavia to have sailed for Europe with the October fleet. I can only return such services by ever retaining a grateful remembrance of them. Mr. Max, the town surgeon, likewise behaved to us with the most disinterested humanity; he attended every one with the utmost care; for which I could not prevail on him to receive any payment, or to render me any account, or other answer than that it was his duty.

CHAPTER XIX.

FROM TIMOR TO BATAVIA.

Thursday, August 20th.—From Coupang we steered N.W. by W., having a moderate breeze at S.E. with fair weather.

Saturday, 22d.—At daylight we saw the island Flores to the northward. We steered along the south side of Flores, mostly with light winds and

* The *Toogetooge* and the *Roomee* are described in Captain Cook's last voyage.

hazy weather, so that we did not constantly keep sight of the coast.

Tuesday, 25th.—At noon we were off Toorus island, which bore N.W. by N., three or four leagues distant. There is a curious high peak on the S.W. part: the land near the shore is low and woody.

On the 27th, at noon, we were near the entrance of the Straits of Mangaryn, which not appearing so open and clear as represented in the map, I steered for the Straits of Sapi, intending to pass through ; but was obliged to give up this plan, by strong currents setting to the S.E., which there was not sufficient wind to enable us to stem. I therefore again stood for the Straits of Mangaryn, which we ran through in the afternoon of the 29th, being favoured with a fresh breeze from the S.S.E. On the Flores side, there are many good harbours and bays, where vessels may anchor ; but the country hereabouts appears burnt up and desolate.

When we had passed the straits, we kept to the westward, running along the north side of the island Sumbawa, where there is a very high mountain near the coast ; at the foot of which, I am informed, are many runs of good water, conveniently situated for ships to supply themselves.

In the night of the 31st, several prows were rowing about us, on which account we kept all night under arms.

Thursday, Sept. 3d.—This and the two following days we were sailing along the north side of the island Lombock, on which is a high mountain. Most of the islands in this route are distinguished by high mountains. Lombock appears to be well clothed with wood. In the nights we saw fires placed on the high lands, at a distance from the coast.

Sunday, 6th.—In the afternoon we saw the high land of Cape Sandana, which is the N.E. part of Java. The next day we were off Cape Sandana, which is a low cape projecting from the high land already mentioned.

We steered to the westward, along the coast of Java ; and on the 10th, at noon, we anchored off Passourwang, a Dutch settlement on the coast of Java, in two fathoms ; distant from the shore half a league : the entrance of the river bearing S.W. The coast hereabouts is so shoal, that large ships are obliged to anchor three or four miles from the land. As soon as we were at anchor, I got in my boat and went on shore. The banks of the river, near the entrance, were mud, on which grew a few mangrove bushes. Among them we saw hogs running, and many were lying dead in the mud, which caused a most intolerable stench, and made me heartily repent having come here, but after proceeding about a mile up the river, the course of which was serpentine, we found a very pleasant country, and landed at a small and well-constructed fort ; where I was received in a friendly and polite manner by M. Adrian Van Rye, the commandant. By the return of the boat, I sent on board a small bullock, and other provisions. I likewise took a pilot to conduct us to Sourabya.

The houses at Passourwang are neatly built, and the country appears to be well cultivated. The produce of this settlement is rice, of which they export large quantities. There are but few Dutch here: the Javanese are numerous, and their chief lives with considerable splendour. They have good roads, and posts are established along the coast ; and it appears to be a busy and well-regulated settlement.

The next day, about noon, we sailed ; and on the 12th, in the evening, anchored in Sourabya road, in seven fathoms : distance from the shore one mile. We found riding here, seven square-rigged and several smaller vessels.

It was too late when we anchored to send a boat on shore. The next morning, before daylight, three guard-boats stationed themselves near us, and I was informed that I must not land or send a boat on shore. This restriction, I learnt from the officer of the guard boats, was in conformity to general orders concerning all strange vessels on their first arrival. At nine in the forenoon, leave came off for us to land, and soon after the guard-boats quitted us.

I was received on shore with great civility and friendship by the governor, or Opperhooft, M. Ant. Barkay, and the commandant of the troops, M. de Bose. By these gentlemen I was hospitably entertained, and advised to remain till the 16th, when some vessels were to sail, with whom I might keep company, which they recommended on account of pirates.

Sourabya is one of the most pleasant places I ever saw. It is situated on the banks of a river, and is a mile and a half distant from the sea shore, so that only the flag-staff can be seen from the road. The river is navigable up to the town for vessels of 100 tons burthen, and the bank on one side is made convenient for tracking. The Chinese carry on a considerable trade here, and have a town or camp on the side of the river opposite to Sourabya. The country near the town is flat, and the soil light, so that they plough with a single bullock or buffalo (karrabow). The interior parts of the country, near the mountains, are infested with a breed of fierce tigers, which makes travelling inland very dangerous. They have here a breed of horses, which are small, but they are handsome and strong.

The Javanese in this neighbourhood are numerous. M. Barkay and M. de Bose took me with them to pay a visit to two of the principal natives, whom we found attended by a number of men armed with pikes, in great military order. We were entertained with a concert of music ; the instruments were gongs, drums, and a fiddle with two strings. I hired a pilot here to carry us to Batavia.

On the 17th, we sailed from Sourabya, in company with three prows. At noon, we anchored at Crissey, which is a town with a small fort belonging to the Dutch. We remained here about two hours and then weighed.

The navigation through the Straits of Madura is so intricate, that, with the little opportunity I had, I am unable to undertake a description of it. The next day (September 18th) having passed the straits, we bore away to the westward, along the coast of Java, in company with the prows before mentioned. We had regular soundings all the way to Samarang, off which place we anchored on the 22d in the afternoon. The shoalness of the coast here, makes the road of Samarang very inconvenient, both on account of the great distance that large ships (of which there were several in the road) are obliged to lie from the shore, and of the landing, which is in a river that cannot be entered before half-flood. This river resembles the one at Passourwang, the shores being low, with man-

sive dead animals lying about. I was met at the landing-place by the equipage-master, and he furnished me with a carriage to carry me to the governor, whose residence is about two miles from the town of Samarang. I requested, and obtained leave, to have our wants supplied, which were, to recruit our provisions, and to get a new main-mast, having sprung ours in the passage from Sourabya. Samarang is a fortified town, surrounded by a wall and ditch; and is the most considerable settlement, next to Batavia, that the Dutch have in Java. Here is a very good hospital, and a public school, chiefly for teaching the mathematics. They have likewise a theatre. Provisions are remarkably cheap here, beef being at ten doits per pound, and the price of a fowl twelve doits.

I experienced great civility from some of the gentlemen at Samarang, particularly from M. le Baron de Bose, a merchant, brother to the M. de Bose, commandant of the troops at Sourabya: and from M. Abegg, the surgeon of the hospital, to whom we were indebted for advice and medicines, for which he would not consent to receive payment. On the 26th, we sailed from Samarang: and with us, a galley mounting six swivels, which the governor had directed to accompany us to Batavia.

On the first of October we anchored in Batavia road, where we found riding, a Dutch ship of war, and twenty sail of Dutch East India ships, besides many smaller vessels.

CHAPTER XX.

OCCURRENCES AT BATAVIA, AND PASSAGE THENCE TO ENGLAND.

In the afternoon, at four o'clock, I went on shore, and landed at a house by the river, where strangers first stop and give an account who they are, whence they come, &c. From this place, a Malay gentleman took me in a carriage to the Sabandar, Mr. Englehard, whose house was in the environs of the city, on the side nearest the shipping. The Sabandar is the officer with whom all strangers are obliged to transact their business: at least, the whole must go through his hands. With him, I went to pay my respects to the governor-general, who received me with great civility. I acquainted his excellency with my situation, and requested my people might be taken care of, and that we should be allowed to take a passage to Europe in the first ship that sailed. I likewise desired permission to sell the schooner and launch. All this his excellency told me should be granted. I then took leave, and returned with the Sabandar, who wrote down the particulars of my wants, in order to form from them a regular petition, to be presented to the council the next day. I had brought from the governor of Coupang, directed for the governor-general at Batavia, the account of my voyage and misfortune, translated into Dutch, from an account that I had given to Mr. Van Este. So attentive had they been at Timor to every thing that related to us.

There is a large hotel at Batavia, fitted up purposely for the accommodation of strangers, who are not allowed to reside at any other place. It is situated near the great river, in a part of the city that is reckoned the most airy and healthy. Nevertheless, I found the air hot and suffocating, and was taken ill in the night with a violent pain in my head. The next morning, at nine, the council sat, and I attended, accompanied by the Sabandar; and was informed that the council had complied with all I had requested.

When I returned to the hotel, my head-ach increased, and a violent fever came on. I sent to acquaint the Sabandar of my situation, and was soon after attended by the head surgeon of the town hospital, Mr. Aanzorp; by whose care and skill, in less than 24 hours, the fever considerably abated, but a severe head-ach continued. I had an invitation from the governor-general to dine with him; which, of course, I was obliged to decline.

I hired a carriage, which cost three dollars per day, for the benefit of taking an airing. My lodgings at the hotel were so close and hot, that I desired the Sabandar to apply to the governor-general, for leave to hire a house in the country; which request his excellency not only immediately complied with, but gave directions for my being accommodated at the house of the physician or surgeon-general, Mr. Sparling.

One of my people, Thomas Hall, being ill with a flux, I obtained leave for him to be sent to the country hospital, which is a convenient airy building.

Tuesday, 6th.—This morning, at sunrise, I left the hotel, and was carried to Mr. Sparling's house, about four miles distant from the city, and near the convalescent hospital, which at this time had also sick men in it, the whole number of patients amounting to 800. I found every thing prepared for my comfort and convenience. Mr. Sparling would suffer me to take no medicine, though I had still considerable fever with head-ach: but I found so much relief from the difference of the air, that in the evening I was able to accompany Mr. Sparling on a visit to the governor-general, at one of his country seats; where we found many ladies, all dressed in the Malay fashion, some of them richly ornamented with jewels. I had invitations from several gentlemen, and some very kindly pressed me to make their country houses my abode, till my health should be re-established.

My indisposition increasing, Mr. Sparling advised me to quit Batavia as speedily as possible, and represented the necessity of it to the governor-general. I was informed from his excellency, that the homeward bound ships were so much crowded, that there would be no possibility of all my people going in one ship, and that they could be accommodated no other way than by dividing them into different ships. Seeing, therefore, that a separation was unavoidable, I determined to follow the advice of the physician, and, as a packet was appointed to sail for Europe on the 16th instant, I sent to request of the governor that I might be allowed to take a passage in her for myself, and as many of my people as they were able to receive. In answer to this, I was acquainted that myself and two more could be accommodated in the packet, she being too small to admit a greater number; but that I might rest assured of passages being provided for those that remained, by the earliest opportunities.

Friday, 9th.—This day, anchored in the road, the General Elliot, an English ship, commanded by Captain Lloyd. In the Straits of Banca, he had met with some boats belonging to the East India Company's ship Vansittart, that was lost in the Straits of Billaton, by having struck on a rock that went through her bottom. Captain Wilson, who commanded the Vansittart, I was informed, had just finished a survey of those straits, and was hoisting his boat out, when the ship struck. Immediately on receiving the intelligence, Captain Lloyd, in the General Elliot, and another ship in company, called the Nonsuch, sailed for the wreck. They found the ship had been burnt down to the water's edge by the Malays. They, however, saved 40 chests of treasure, out of 55, which were said to have been on board. Most of the ship's company were saved: one man only was lost in the ship, and five others in a small boat were missing, who were supposed to have taken some of the treasure.—The greater part of the people went with Captain Wilson to China, and some were with Captain Lloyd.

Saturday, 16th.—This morning, the Resource was sold by public auction: the custom at Batavia, is to begin high, and to lower the price, till some person bids; and the first bidder is the buyer. She was accordingly put up at 2000 rix-dollars, but, to my great disappointment, no one offered to purchase before the auctioneer had lowered the demand to 295 rix-dollars, for which price she was sold; the purchaser being an Englishman, Captain John Eddie, who commanded an English ship from Bengal. If no strangers had been present at the sale, I imagine they would have let her run down to 200 dollars, in which case I should have had no alternative.

The launch likewise was sold. The services she had rendered us, made me feel great reluctance at parting with her; which I would not have done, if I could have found a convenient opportunity of getting her conveyed to Europe.

Little as the schooner had sold for, I found I was in danger of having the sum lessened; for the Sabandar informed me, that, by an order of the council, there was a duty on the sale of all vessels. With this demand I would by no means comply; for I thought I had sufficiently suffered, in sustaining a loss of 705 rix-dollars out of 1000, by the purchase and sale of the vessel, she having cost 1000 rix-dollars.

This day, Thomas Hall, whom I had sent to be taken care of at the hospital, died. He had been ill of a flux from the time of our arrival at Timor.

Monday, 12th.—I agreed with the captain of the packet for a passage to Europe, for myself, my clerk, and a servant. The Sabandar informed me, it was necessary that my officers and people should be examined before a notary, respecting the loss of the Bounty, as otherwise the governor and council were not legally authorized to detain her, if she should be found in any of the Dutch settlements. They were therefore, at my desire, examined; and afterwards made affidavit before the governor and council at the Stadt-house.

My officers complaining to me of the unreasonableness of some tradesmen's bills, I spoke to the Sabandar. A bill of 51 dollars for five hats, he reduced to 30 dollars, and in other articles made proportionable deductions.

Paper money is the currency of Batavia, and is so understood in all bargains. At this time, paper was at 28 per cent. discount: there is likewise a difference in the value of the ducatoon, which at Batavia is 80 stivers, and in Holland only 63 stivers: this occasions a loss of 21¼ per cent. on

remittance of money. It therefore follows, that if any person at Batavia remits money by bills of exchange to Europe, they lose by the discount and the exchange 49½ per cent.

Those who have accounts to pay, and can give unexceptionable bills on Europe, will find a considerable saving by negociating their bills with private people; who are glad to give for them a premium of 20 per cent. at the least. This discovery, I made somewhat too late to profit by.

One of the greatest difficulties that strangers have to encounter, is, their being obliged to live at the hotel. This hotel was formerly two houses, which by doors of communication have been made one. It is in the middle of a range of buildings, more calculated for a cold country than for such a climate as Batavia. There is no free circulation of air; and what is equally bad, it is always very dirty; and there is great want of attendance. What they call cleaning the house, is another nuisance; for they never use any water to cool it or to lay the dust, but sweep daily with brooms, in such a manner, that those in the house are almost suffocated by a cloud of dust.

The months of December and January are reckoned the most unhealthy of the year, the heavy rains being then set in.——The account of the seasons, as given to me here, I believe may be relied on.

The middle of November, the west monsoon begins, and rain.

December and January.—Continual rain with strong westerly wind.

February.—Westerly wind. Towards the end of this month the rain begins to abate.

March.—Intervals of fine weather. Wind westerly.

April.—In this month the east monsoon begins. Weather generally fine, with showers of rain.

May. East monsoon fixed. Showery.

June and July. Clear weather. Strong east wind.

August and September. Wind more moderate.

October. In this month, the wind begins to be variable, with showers of rain.

The current is said always to run with the wind. Nevertheless I found the reverse in sailing from Timor to Java. Between the end of October and the beginning of the ensuing year, no Dutch ship bound for Europe is allowed to sail from Batavia, for fear of being near the Mauritius, at the time of the hurricanes, which are frequent there in December and January.

My illness prevented me from gaining much knowledge of Batavia. Of their public buildings, I saw nothing that gave me so much satisfaction as their country hospital for seamen. It is a large commodious and airy building, about four miles from the town, close to the side of the river, or rather in the river: for the ground on which it stands has, by labour, been made an island of, and the sick are carried there in a boat: each ward is a separate dwelling, and the different diseases are properly classed. They have sometimes 1400 patients in it: at this time there were 800, but more than half of these were recovered and fit for service, of whom 300 were destined for the fleet that was to sail for Europe. I went through most of the wards, and there appeared great care and attention. The sheets, bedding, and linen, of the sick were perfectly neat and clean. The house of the physician, Mr. Sparling, who has the management of the hospital, is at one extremity of the building : and here it was that I resided. To the attention and care of this gentleman, for which he would receive no payment, I am probably indebted for my life.

The hospital in the town is well attended, but the situation is so ill chosen, that it certainly would be the saving of many lives to build one in its stead up the river ; which might be done with great advantage, as water carriage is so easy and convenient. A great neglect in some of the commanders of the shipping here, was suffering their people to go dirty, and frequently without frock, shirt, or any thing to cover their bodies ; which, besides being a public nuisance, must probably be productive of ill health in the most robust constitution.

The governor-general gave me leave to lodge all my people at the country hospital, which I thought a great advantage, and with which they were perfectly satisfied. The officers, however, at their own request, remained in the town.

The time fixed for the sailing of the packet approaching, I settled my accounts with the Sabandar, leaving open the victualling account, to be closed by Mr. Fryer, the master, previous to his departure ; whom I likewise authorised to supply the men and officers left under his command, with one month's pay, to enable them to purchase clothing for their passage to England.

I had been at great pains to bring living plants from Timor, in six tubs ; which contained jacks, nancas, karambolas, namnams, jambos, and three thriving bread-fruit plants. These I thought might be serviceable at the Cape of Good Hope, if brought no farther : but I had the mortification of being obliged to leave them all at Batavia. I took these plants on board at Coupang, on the 20th of August : they had experienced a passage of forty-two days to my arrival here. The bread-fruit plants died to the root, and sprouted afresh from thence. The karambolas, jacks, nancas, and namnams, I had raised from the seed, and they were in fine order. No judgment can hence be formed of the success of transporting plants, as in the present trial they had many disadvantages.

This morning, Friday 16th, before sun-rise, I embarked on board the Vlydte packet, commanded by Captain Peter Couvret, bound for Middleburgh. With me likewise embarked Mr. John Samuel, clerk, and John Smith, seaman. Those of our company who staid behind, the governor promised me should follow in the first ships, and be as little divided as possible.——At seven o'clock the packet weighed, and sailed out of the road.

On the 18th we spoke the Rambler, an American brig, belonging to Boston, bound to Batavia. After passing the Straits of Sunda, we steered to the north of the Cocos Isles. These islands, Captain Couvret informed me, are full of cocoa-nut trees : there is no anchorage near them, but good landing for boats.

In the passage to the Cape of Good Hope there occurred nothing worth remark. I cannot, however, forbear noticing the Dutch manner of navigating. They steer by true compass, or rather endeavour so to do, by means of a small moveable central card, which they set to the meridian : and whenever they discover the variation has altered

2½ degrees since the last adjustment, they again correct the central card. This is steering within a quarter of a point, without aiming at greater exactness. The officer of the watch likewise corrects the course for lee-way, by his own judgment, before it is marked down in the log board. They heave no log : I was told that the Company do not allow it. Their manner of computing their run, is by means of a measured distance of forty feet along the ship's side : they take notice of any remarkable patch of froth, when it is abreast the foremost end of the measured distance, and count half seconds till the mark of froth is abreast the after end. With the number of half seconds thus obtained, they divide the number forty-eight, taking the product for the rate of sailing in geographical miles in one hour, or the number of Dutch miles in four hours.

It is not usual to make any allowance to the sun's declination, on account of being on a different meridian from that for which the tables are calculated ; they in general compute with the numbers just as they are found in the table. From all this it is not difficult to conceive the reason why the Dutch are frequently above ten degrees out in their reckoning. Their passages likewise are considerably lengthened by not carrying a sufficient quantity of sail.

December 16th, in the afternoon we anchored in Table Bay. The next morning I went on shore, and waited on his Excellency M. Vander Graaf, who received me in the most polite and friendly manner. The Guardian, commanded by Lieut. Riou, had left the Cape about eight days before, with cattle and stores for Port Jackson. This day anchored in Table Bay, the Astrée, a French frigate, commanded by the Count de St. Rivel, from the Isle of France, on board of which ship was the late governor, the Chevalier d'Entrecasteaux. Other ships that arrived during my stay at the Cape, were, a French forty gun frigate, an East India ship, and a brig of the same nation : likewise two other French ships, with slaves from the coast of Mosambique, bound to the West Indies : a Dutch packet from Europe, after a four months' passage : and the Harpy, a South Sea whaler, with 500 barrels of spermaceti, and 400 of seal and other oils. There is a standing order from the Dutch East India Company, that no person who takes a passage from Batavia for Europe, in any of their ships, shall be allowed to leave the ship before she arrives at her intended port ; according to which regulation, I must have gone to Holland in the packet. Of this I was not informed till I was taking leave of the governor-general, at Batavia, when it was too late for him to give the captain an order to permit me to land in the channel. He however desired I would make use of his name to Governor Vander Graaf, who readily complied with my request, and gave the necessary orders to the captain of the packet, a copy of which his Excellency gave to me ; and at the same time, recommendatory letters to people of consequence in Holland, in case I should be obliged to proceed so far.

I left a letter at the Cape of Good Hope, to be forwarded to Governor Phillips, at Port Jackson, by the first opportunity ; containing a short account of my voyage, with a descriptive list of the pirates : and from Batavia I had written to Lord

Cornwallis ; so that every part of India will be prepared to receive them.

We sailed from the Cape, on Saturday, 2nd January, 1790, in company with the Astrée French frigate. The next morning neither ship nor land was in sight. On the 15th, we passed in sight of the island St. Helena. The 21st, we saw the Island Ascension. On the 10th of February, the wind being at N. E., blowing fresh, our sails were covered with a fine orange-coloured dust. Fuego, the westernmost of the Cape de Verd islands, and the nearest land to us, on that day at noon bore N.E. by E. ½ E., distance 140 leagues. On the 13th of March, we saw the Bill of Portland, and on the evening of the next day, Sunday March the 14th, I left the packet, and was landed at Portsmouth, by an Isle of Wight boat.

Those of my officers and people whom I left at Batavia, were provided with passages in the earliest ships ; and at the time we parted, were apparently in good health. Nevertheless they did not all live to quit Batavia. Mr. Elphinstone, master's mate, and Peter Linkletter, seaman, died within a fortnight after my departure ; the hardships they had experienced having rendered them unequal to cope with so unhealthy a climate as that of Batavia. The remainder embarked on board the Dutch fleet for Europe, and arrived safe at this country, except Robert Lamb, who died on the passage, and Mr. Ledward, the surgeon, who has not yet been heard of. Thus of nineteen who were forced by the mutineers into the launch, it has pleased God that twelve should surmount the difficulties and dangers of the voyage, and live to revisit their native country.

APPENDIX;

CONTAINING

ADDITIONAL PARTICULARS RESPECTING THE MUTINY ON BOARD THE BOUNTY, AND A RELATION OF THE FATE OF THE MUTINEERS, AND OF THE SETTLEMENT IN PITCAIRN'S ISLAND.*

CAPTAIN BLIGH'S account of his voyage has been given precisely as he published it, in 1792, without any alteration, saving the suppression of those parts where he records his observations of the latitude, longitude, bearings and soundings of particular places, of no interest to any but the mariner, and even to him now rendered almost, if not quite useless, by subsequent and more accurate surveys.

The superiority of the pleasure derived from reading a journal of facts, recorded day by day while the *immediate* impression remains, over a formal narrative, is so great, as to render it very desirable that the original should be presented to the public, rather than a vamped and tinselled substitute. In many cases however, the original is not adapted for that purpose ; but the present is far otherwise, and we trace the daily progress of the skilful mariner, on whose life the existence of his fellow sufferers depended, with earnest hope and eager expectation. His narrative is like a moving picture ; full of horrors, it is true, but of horrors that fix our gaze upon them.

Captain Bligh's character stood deservedly high in his profession, in which he afterwards rose to the rank of a flag officer, but his temper was infirm, and when under its influence he suffered himself to use language both to his crew and officers, which it is now surprising to believe was not *quite uncommon* at that period, even from gentlemen holding the rank he did, at the time of the mutiny.

Disputes began early between him and his officers and crew, and appear to have originated from the circumstance of the commander combining in his own person, as was usual in small vessels, the offices of captain and purser. Many irritating altercations occurred, which were met by Captain Bligh with much heat of temper, but when passed, though forgotten by him, were remembered by others. His conduct in the voyage out, when his judicious regulations preserved the health of his ship's company in a very trying season, and the remarkable steadiness of his management of his men, when exposed in the boat, and tried to the utmost by their behaviour, even then unruly, prove him to have been not only fully equal, but worthy to command. Six months' relaxation from the strict reins of discipline on the fascinating shores of Otaheite, were not calculated to make the renewed curb sit easy. Disputes again began, and the captain's temper again got the better of him. Christian, who had received kindness from the captain with one hand and insults with the other, took a sudden resolution which he afterwards repented bitterly ; he found ready helpmates, but none rallied round the captain. All save the captain's clerk on the one side, and those whom Christian had, in the first instance, called on, on the other, were for a time paralysed, and slowly took their determination biassed by fear or hatred in all their actions, but none by love, if we except the compassionate sailor who fed the captain with shaddock.

Captain Bligh considered the mutiny as the result of a conspiracy, but no evidence to support that opinion was ever produced ; on the contrary, in a journal kept by Morrison the boatswain's mate, an account of its origin is given, professedly from Christian's own relation, and this is the only distinct narrative of it that has ever been made public. It appears that Christian, feeling himself much aggrieved at the captain's treatment, had formed the resolution of quitting the ship on the evening

* The authorities chiefly relied on are the papers of Capt. Heywood, first made public in 1855 ; the narrative of the voyage of the Pandora, by Mr. Hamilton ; the voyage of the Briton, by Mr. Shillibeer ; and the narrative of Capt. Beechey's voyage in the Blossom.

preceding the mutiny, and for that purpose had provided himself with a stout plank, to which he had fixed several staves. On this frail raft he determined to trust himself, hoping to reach the island of Tofoa; and with this view had, with the assistance of two midshipmen, Stewart and *Hayward*, who were privy to his design, filled a bag with provision. The ship making very little way, prevented him from executing his design. About half past three he lay down to sleep, and at four was roused to take the watch. On going on deck he found his mate, Mr. Hayward, asleep, and the other officer, Mr. Hallett, did not appear. He instantly determined to seize the ship, went forward, spoke to some of the crew he thought he could trust, put arms in their hands, and proceeded as Captain Bligh relates.

This appears from all the various accounts of the evidence on the Court Martial, afterwards held on the mutineers, to have been the true state of the case; but the moral obligation of obedience to discipline in a ship, must have been totally forgotten by both officers and crew, when such a sudden determination was thought capable of execution, and not one soul stepped forward to oppose it.

When the boat containing Captain Bligh and his companions was cast off, there remained on board the Bounty—

FLETCHER CHRISTIAN, Master's Mate, and acting Lieutenant, afterwards murdered at Pitcairn's Island.

PETER HEYWOOD, Midshipman, surrendered himself to Captain Edwards of the Pandora; was tried, condemned, pardoned, and afterwards attained the rank of captain in the service.

EDWARD YOUNG, Midshipman, died at Pitcairn's Island.

GEORGE STEWART, do., drowned on board the Pandora.

CHARLES CHURCHILL, Master-at-Arms, murdered by Thompson, at Otaheite.

JOHN MILLS, Gunner's Mate, murdered at Pitcairn's Island.

JAMES MORRISON, Boatswain's Mate, tried, condemned, and pardoned.

THOMAS BURKITT, Seaman, tried, condemned, and executed.

MATTHEW QUINTAL, do., put to death by Adams and Young at Pitcairn's Island.

JOHN SUMNER, do., drowned on board the Pandora.

JOHN MILLWARD, do., tried, condemned, and executed.

WILLIAM M'KOY, do., committed suicide at Pitcairn's Island.

HENRY HILLBRANT, do., drowned on board the Pandora.

MICHAEL BYRNE, do., tried and acquitted.

WILLIAM MUSPRAT, do., tried, condemned, and pardoned.

ALEXANDER SMITH (alias JOHN ADAMS), do., died at Pitcairn's Island in 1829.

JOHN WILLIAMS, do., murdered at Pitcairn's Island.

THOMAS ELLISON, do., tried, condemned, and executed.

ISAAC MARTIN, do., murdered at Pitcairn's Island.

RICHARD SKINNER, do., drowned on board the Pandora.

MATTHEW THOMPSON, do., put to death by the natives at Otaheite, for the murder of Churchill.

WILLIAM BROWN, Gardener, murdered at Pitcairn's Island.

JOSEPH COLEMAN, Armourer, tried and acquitted.

CHARLES NORMAN, Carpenter's Mate, do. do.

THOMAS M'INTOSH, Carpenter's Crew, do. do.

When Captain Bligh's boat was cast off, Christian assumed the command of the Bounty; he steered for Toobouai, an island situated in latitude 20° 13′ S., and longitude 149° 35′ W., where they anchored on the 25th May, 1789. All the bread-fruit plants were thrown overboard, and the property of the officers and men sent adrift was divided among the mutineers. Here they intended to form a settlement; but, in consequence of quarrels among themselves, and with the natives, and the want of many things which could be procured at Otaheite, but which could not be obtained at Toobouai, they determined to go to Otaheite, but with no intention of remaining there. On their arrival (on the 6th of June) they told the Otaheiteans that Captain Bligh had fallen in with their old friend Captain Cook, who was engaged in forming a settlement on an island called Why-tootakee, and that Captain Bligh and the rest of the crew had stopped with him; that the command of the vessel had been transferred to Christian, who had been sent to obtain a fresh supply of stores. This story was readily believed by the Otaheiteans, who immediately set about collecting provisions, and in a few days sent on board 312 hogs, 38 goats, 8 dozen of fowls, a bull, and a cow, and a large quantity of bread-fruit, plantains, bananas, and other fruits. Christian peremptorily forbade any person to remain at Otaheite, and his partisans kept so close a watch on those who were suspected of any inclination to leave them, that none could contrive to escape; and as soon as the stores were all on board, they again set sail and returned to Toobouai, where they again went to work to build a fort, but finding it impossible to agree together, it was at last determined to abandon Toobouai, take the ship back to Otaheite, and land all who chose to quit her there. They arrived in Matavai Bay on the 20th of September, when sixteen men were put on shore; the small arms, powder, and stores, were equally divided between the two parties; and on the night of the 21st September, Christian and his companions again set sail, carrying with them seven Otaheitean men, and twelve women. Where they intended to go was not known, but Christian had been heard to say, that he should seek for an uninhabited island, where there was no harbour, and should there run the ship ashore and break her up.

The natives treated their guests with the greatest hospitality, and several of the Englishmen married Otaheitean women, and when they were seized in 1789, many of them had children. Mr. Stewart, in particular, had married the daughter of a chief, who possessed a very large tract of country; and when the Pandora arrived was living with her as a man of property and consequence[*]. Morrison, Heywood, and Stewart, when at Toobouai, had formed a plan of seizing the ship's boat, and escaping to Otaheite, but abandoned the design, finding that the condition of the boat was too bad to give them a chance of success. Morrison now undertook to build a schooner, which, with the assistance of the carpenter, the cooper, and some others, he completed. His object was to reach Batavia in time to join the next fleet bound to Holland, and he and six of his companions actually set sail, but found themselves obliged to return, as their stores proved too small for so long an expedition, and the natives, who did not wish to part with them, refused to give them more. This schooner ac-

[*] The parting of poor Stewart and his wife and child is described in the first missionary voyage of the ship Duff as having been heart-rending. His wife died of a broken heart two months after his departure.

companied the Pandora when she left Otaheite, parted company with her near the Palmerston Islands, but arrived safely at Samarang, in Java, after a voyage in which the crew suffered dreadfully from want of water and provisions. She was an admirable sailer, and was afterwards employed in the sea-otter trade, and subsequently bought at Canton by the late Captain Broughton, to assist in the survey of the coast of Tartary.

Stewart and Heywood did not join Morrison in this expedition, considering it much better to remain at Otaheite, where it was certain that some European vessel would touch before a long time elapsed.

When Captain Bligh arrived in England and the account of the mutiny was given to the world, a universal feeling of sympathy for the sufferers, and of indignation against the mutineers, took possession of the public mind. It was felt, and justly, that any breach of that discipline which is the main stay of the navy, the bulwark of Britain, is deserving of severe punishment; and that the perpetrators of so flagrant a violation of the first of a seaman's duties should be pursued even to the uttermost parts of the earth, and brought back to answer for their crime to their injured country. The Admiralty were fully possessed of these sentiments, and determined to make every effort to secure the offenders: with this view the Pandora frigate, Capt. Edward Edwards, mounting twenty-four guns, and manned by a crew of 124 men, was commissioned, and so well victualled that, to use the expression of Mr. Hamilton the surgeon, who has written an amusing, though rather coarse account, of a most disastrous voyage, "they were obliged to eat a hole in their bread before they had room to lie down." They sailed in August, 1790, with orders to proceed in the first instance to Otaheite, and, not finding the mutineers there, to visit the different groups of the Society and Friendly Islands, and the others in the neighbouring parts of the Pacific; using their best endeavours to seize and bring home in confinement the whole or such part of the delinquents as they might be able to discover.

On the voyage the crew suffered much from an infectious fever, and at one time thirty-five men were laid up sick in their hammocks. An alarm of a Spanish frigate bearing down, put them to much inconvenience from the lumbered state of the vessel; but when the bulk-heads were all down and the ship cleared for action, the supposed enemy turned out to be a good friend, his Majesty's ship the Shark.

They touched at Rio Janeiro, where Captain Edwards was entertained by the viceroy. His palace was handsome, and its interior decorations were very beautiful and singularly appropriate. In various apartments, paintings on the ceilings displayed all the objects of natural history peculiar to the country. In one apartment appeared the quadrupeds, in another the fishes, in a third the birds and shells were displayed in groups and borderings. This elegant mode of adorning rooms is well worthy of imitation.

The voyage from Rio was prosperous, and the vessel arrived in Matavai Bay on the 23rd of March, 1791. Immediately on her arrival, Coleman, the armourer of the Bounty, put off in a canoe, and went on board; he was quickly followed by Stewart and Heywood, who voluntarily surrendered themselves; they, however, met with a very ungracious reception from Captain Edwards, who ordered them to be put in irons immediately. A party was sent after the rest of the mutineers, who were soon secured; and the whole were lodged together in a small prison erected for the purpose on the quarter-deck, the only entrance to which was by a scuttle in the roof, about eighteen inches square, and confined with both legs and feet in irons. "The prisoners' wives," says Mr. Hamilton, in his account of the Pandora's voyage, "visited the ship daily, and brought their children, who were permitted to be carried to their unhappy fathers. To see the poor captives in irons weeping over their tender offspring, was too moving a scene for any feeling heart. Their wives brought them ample supplies of every delicacy that the country afforded while we lay there, and behaved with the greatest fidelity and affection to them."

Sixteen men had left the Bounty at Otaheite; fourteen were now on board the Pandora; the remaining two had both died violent deaths. One of these, Churchill, was murdered by his companion Thompson, for some insult he had received; and Thompson was in return stoned to death by the natives, the friends of the murdered man, who had attained the rank of a chief.

The Pandora set sail on the 8th May, and proceeded to make a search, prolonged for three months, among the various groups of islands, but without meeting with any trace of Christian and his companions, except on one of the Palmerston Islands, where a mast and some spars belonging to the Bounty were found. On the 29th of August they arrived off New Holland, and ran along the barrier reef, a boat being sent out to look for an opening, but in the night the ship struck, and she immediately began to fill with water; all hands were employed at the pumps and baling from the hatchways, but to no effect; the leak increased, and the ship beat over the reef into the deep water on the other side. It was evident that she was sinking, and the people took to the boats. Three only of the prisoners had been liberated to work at the pumps, but the prayers of the others to be allowed to assist were totally disregarded; the guard over them had been doubled, and all would have been drowned if the armourer, either by accident or from design, had not dropped his keys into the prison, and with them they set themselves free; one of the sailors, at the risk of his life, held on by the coombings, and drew out the long shackle bolts, and thus all but four, who miserably perished, saved themselves at the moment that the ship went down, and when the whole deck was under water. Stewart was one of those who were thus unfortunately lost.

All who had contrived to escape made for a sandy key about three miles from the wreck, and on mustering the hands it was found that 89 of the ship's company and ten of the mutineers, were saved; but thirty-one of the ship's company, and four of the mutineers, had gone down with the wreck.

The survivors were now distributed in the boats, and after a miserable voyage arrived at Coupang on the 15th of August, where they remained three weeks. Here the prisoners were again confined in irons in the castle, and were treated in the same way at Batavia, whither they were transported in a Dutch ship. From thence they set sail in a Dutch Indiaman, but falling in with the Gorgon man-of-war at the Cape, they were transferred to that vessel, and arrived at Spithead on the 19th June, 1792.

The Court-Martial met on the 12th of September, and after an investigation which lasted six days, gave their judgment that the charges had been proved against Peter Heywood, James Morrison, Thomas Ellison, Thomas Burkitt, John Millward, and William Musprat; but recommended Heywood and Morrison to mercy. Norman, Coleman, M'Intosh, and Byrne, all of whom had expressed their desire to go into the boat, were acquitted. Eventually, a free pardon was granted to Heywood, Morrison, and Musprat; but the other three suffered the penalty of their crime, and were hung on board the Brunswick, on the 29th of October.

The case of Heywood was particularly hard, and was generally so considered. He had done no act which could be construed into assisting in the mutiny; but his case is an instance which should never be forgotten by the seaman, of that salutary rule, which determines that he who does not oppose a mutiny, makes himself a party to it. There were, however, so many extenuating circumstances in Heywood's case, as almost to take it out of the reach of even this strict interpretation. He was only fifteen years of age, and this was his first voyage; waked from his sleep by the news of a mutiny, he came on deck, found the captain a prisoner, heard two of the officers (Hayward and Fryer, who were afterwards forced into the boat) terrified at the idea of being turned adrift, entreat to be left in the ship, and saw that no effort was made by his superiors or any other to oppose the mutineers. He at first very naturally determined rather to risk himself in the ship than in the boat, of whose safety he despaired; but he changed this determination, and had with Stewart gone to his berth to get some things together, when, by order of the mutineers, the two young men were confined below, and not permitted to come upon deck till the boat with Captain Bligh had put off. All these circumstances were duly appreciated; Mr. Heywood was permitted, against the usual practice in such cases, to resume his profession,* in which his career was prosperous and honourable. He saw much hard service, and attained the rank of captain. He died in the year 1825.

It is now time to return to Christian, and pursue his unfortunate career. All the accounts of his proceedings and of the fate of his companions, are derived from Alexander Smith, or as he afterwards called himself, though from what cause is not known, John Adams. His varying statements to the different persons who saw him at Pitcairn's Island regarding Christian, though apparently not very consistent, may perhaps be both true, especially as no motive for falsehood is apparent. To Captains Staines and Pipon, who first visited him, he stated that Christian was never happy, that he appeared full of shame and misery, after the desperate act he had performed; and that on the voyage to Pitcairn's Island, he shut himself up in his cabin, scarcely ever appeared, and when he did,

seemed sunk in the deepest melancholy: yet he told Captain Beechey that Christian was always cheerful; that his example was of the greatest service in exciting his companions to labour; that he was naturally of a happy ingenuous disposition, and won the good opinion and respect of all who served under him. It does not seem improbable that before he had effected his object, and whilst he was in continual dread of seizure by some British vessel, doubts and fear might cloud his mind, and deaden his spirit, yet that when he found himself as he believed free from all danger and in the full command of those from whom he exacted and received obedience, he should become all that Adams stated him to be to Captain Beechey.

It has generally been supposed that he was a prey to remorse, and that this feeling continually weighing upon and irritating his mind, rendered him morose and savage, and that the indulgence of such feelings cost him his life. This idea was grounded upon Captain Bligh's statement in his narration, "that when he reproached Christian with his ingratitude, he replied, 'That is what it is, Mr. Bligh; I am in hell, I am in hell!'" and upon Adams's statement of his conduct on the voyage to Pitcairn's Island. The evidence on the Court Martial shows that Captain Bligh was quite mistaken in the words of Christian and their import. The master, Mr. Fryer, in his evidence stated that on coming on deck he said to Christian, "Consider what you are about," to which he replied, "Hold your tongue, sir! I have been in hell for weeks past: Captain Bligh has brought all this on himself;" alluding to the frequent quarrels that they had had, and the abuse he had received from Captain Bligh. With respect to Christian's seclusion and apparent melancholy on the subsequent voyage, that has already been noticed and an explanation attempted.

Again, it has been stated that Christian's own act, in forcibly taking away the wife of one of the Otaheitans, was the occasion of his death; that he was shot by the injured husband. It will be seen in the subsequent narration, that this was not the case; that Williams and not Christian was the offending party, and that his crime was the immediate, though not the only cause, of a general insurrection of the black men against the whites, in which Christian fell; not a single victim, but with others. It is also worthy of remark, that on the visit of the English to Pitcairn's Island the young natives on being questioned concerning religion, said it had been first taught by *Christian's* order. The mid-day prayer which they said he appointed is remarkable: "I will arise and go to my father and say unto him, Father, I have sinned against heaven and before thee, and am no more worthy to be called thy son." This prayer, or rather confession, they said Christian had appointed to be said every day at noon, and that the practice was never neglected.

All this tends to prove that Christian's feelings were more those of healthy repentance than morbid remorse.

From this digression we will now return to our narrative.

When Christian left Otaheite, there were on board, besides himself, eight of the most desperate of the mutineers, and six men and twelve

---

* Lord Hood, who sat as President on his trial, received him as a midshipman on board the Victory.

women, natives of Otaheite and Toobouai. His object was to seek out an uninhabited island, out of the track of voyagers, where he intended to break up his vessel, and live with his companions secluded from the world. He fell in with an island first discovered by Captain Carteret, and named by him Pitcairn's Island. It was by him laid down 3 degrees of longitude out of its true position, which is 25° 4′ S. lat., and 130° 25′ W. long.

Here Christian and his companions ran the ship on the rocks, and after getting out every thing useful, set her on fire. The English divided the whole island among them, reserving nothing for the Otaheiteans, whom they treated as servants. They, however, lived together peaceably for two years, built houses for themselves, and cultivated the ground; but a quarrel now broke out between the white and the black men. Williams, one of the Englishmen, had lost his wife, who fell from the rocks while gathering birds' eggs; and he now insisted on having another wife, or leaving the island in one of the ship's boats which had been preserved. As he was a useful man, the English wished to keep him, and made one of the black men give up his wife. The blacks determined on revenge, and laid a plot to murder all the English. Their plan was discovered by the women, who were more attached to the whites than to their own countrymen, and the affair ended in the death of two of the natives, who were treacherously killed in the woods by their companions on a promise of pardon for themselves.

Another interval of quiet now took place, but the tyranny of their masters again drove the Otaheiteans to rebellion. Christian, Williams, and Mills, fell victims to this attack; Quintal and M'Koy fled to the mountains; Young was saved by the women; and Smith, or as he now called himself, Adams, after being wounded, made his peace with the natives. After this execution, the Otaheiteans proceeded to choose wives for themselves, from the widows of the murdered men; but violent disputes arose, and in the end, all the native men fell by the hands of the women, except one who was shot by Young. The men who had fled to the mountains, now returned, and the four, Adams, Young, M'Koy, and Quintal, lived peaceably for some years.

M'Koy, who was a Scotchman, and could not forget his beloved whiskey, was continually trying experiments on the *tee* root, and at last succeeded in manufacturing a spirituous liquor; the consequence of this was, that he and Quintal were constantly intoxicated, and in his own case this proceeded so far as to produce delirium, and in one of the fits he threw himself from a cliff, and was killed on the spot. This was about 1798.

In the course of next year Quintal's wife was killed from a fall from the rocks, and nothing would satisfy him but the wife of one of his companions, although there were several unmarried women to choose from; Young and Adams would not give up their wives, and in revenge Quintal attempted to murder them. His design was prevented, but he swore he would carry it into execution. Young and Adams now considered themselves justified in putting Quintal to death, to secure their own lives; and accordingly they executed their purpose by cutting him down with a hatchet.

Two men alone were now left of all who landed on the island; their situation, and the dreadful scenes they had witnessed—scenes of guilt which entailed their own punishment, seem to have had their due effect. Young, who was of a respectable family, was tolerably educated, as Adams, who was a man of considerable ability, both applied themselves in earnest to manage the little settlement with regularity and order. They studied the bible, and from its pages learned and taught the good lessons of correct life in this world, and the steadfast hope of a happier future. They read the church prayers every Sunday, and instructed the children. Young died about a year after Quintal, and Adams was now left the solitary survivor. He steadily pursued the good course he had begun, and was looked up to by all as their chief; he was their friend, adviser, comforter, instructor, and governor. He regulated every thing, and under his rule they prospered.

Thus they lived on, unknown to the world, but happy in their own society, and pure from the follies and wickedness which disturb the tranquillity of others, till the year 1808 (eighteen years from the foundation of the settlement), when an American vessel, the Topaz, Capt. Folger, touched at the island. Capt. Folger was astonished at discovering the descendants of the mutinous crew of the Bounty, in a race of young people rapidly springing up to manhood, and speaking both English and Otaheitean fluently. He found the little settlement in great order and harmony; their number was about thirty-five, who all looked upon Adams as their father and commander. Captain Folger did not publish any account of his discovery, which was first noticed in the newspapers, and afterwards authenticated by a communication made by him to Lieutenant Fitzmaurice at Valparaiso.

No more was heard of Pitcairn's Island or its inhabitants, till 1814, when two frigates, the Briton* and Tagus, commanded by Sir Thomas Staines, and Captain Pipon, cruising in the Pacific, came to Pitcairn's Island, which, from the error in the charts before alluded to, they were surprised at meeting with in that position. Their astonishment was increased when they were hailed by the crew of a canoe which had put off to them, with "Won't you heave us a rope now?" After some difficulty, for the rope could not be made fast to the canoe, the crew came on board; they were fine young men, about five feet ten inches high, with manly features, partaking somewhat of the Otaheitean cast of countenance, and with long black hair. Their dress was a mantle tied round the waist by a girdle; one end being thrown over the shoulders, and the other hanging to the knees, very much in the fashion of the belted plaid of the ancient Highlanders. They wore straw hats ornamented with feathers. The young women have invariably beautiful teeth, fine eyes, and an open expression of countenance, with an engaging air of simple innocence and sweet sensibility; and their manners, far from displaying the licentiousness common to the inhabitants of other South Sea islands, were simple and unsophisticated, but perfectly modest.

* An account of the voyage of the Briton was published by Mr. Shillibeer, one of her lieutenants.

A few questions put and answered on both sides explained every thing, and one of the visitors proved to be son of Christian, who was the first born on the island, and christened Thursday October, and another was the son of Young. They were naturally delighted and astonished at all they saw in the ship, but were greatly puzzled with the cow, and could not determine whether it was a huge goat or a horned pig, those being the only two quadrupeds they were acquainted with.

They were asked into the cabin to breakfast, but before partaking of the meal, both stood up, and one of them, putting his hands in a posture of devotion, asked a blessing; and they were surprised to observe that this practice, which they said was taught them by Adams, was not attended to by their new acquaintance.

Sir Thomas Staines and Captain Pipon determined to go on shore, which they effected through a considerable surf, which thoroughly wetted them; and when Adams found that there was no intention of seizing him, and that the two captains had come ashore unarmed, he came down to the beach. He was a fine looking old man, between fifty and sixty. He took the captains to his own house, which stood at one end of the square, round which the houses, which all exhibit traces of European construction, are placed; the centre is a green, fenced in for the poultry, of which they have a large stock.

Sir Thomas Staines made a proposal to Adams to go home with him, which he appeared anxious to do; but when he spoke of his desire to his family, a touching scene of sorrow was immediately displayed, and his daughter flinging her arms round his neck, asked him "who would then take care of all his little children?" He could not resist such entreaties, and although it was perhaps the strict duty of the captains to take him, yet they felt themselves justified in waiving its execution in this peculiar case.

They found every thing regulated with the most exact order; every family possessed its separate property, which was well cultivated, John Adams leading the young men and women to work every day. He did not encourage marriage before some property was got together for the support of a family; a rule that was willingly submitted to, and in no case had the slightest tendency to libertinism been observed.

Adams was accustomed to perform the ceremonies of baptism and marriage, but had not ventured to administer the sacrament.

After a stay of two days only, the Briton and Tagus departed, and the next account of the island is that of Captain Beechey, who visited it in 1825; he gives an equally pleasing account of the people or as it may not improperly be described, the family of Pitcairn's Island, and of the patriarch Adams. He found a new-comer among them, a man named Buffett, who had belonged to a whaler, but was so much delighted with the society of this little settlement, that he begged to remain. He was a man of a religious turn of mind, and being possessed of some information made himself very useful both as schoolmaster and clergyman. Captain Beechey attended church, where John Adams read the prayers of the Church of England and Buffett preached, but for fear any of his sermon might be forgotten he repeated it three times over.

All the inhabitants were particular in their religious observances, never omitting their morning and evening prayer and hymn.

The furniture of their houses was very good; they manufactured bedsteads, chests, tables, and stools. The cloth for their sheets and dresses is manufactured from the paper mulberry tree. Their houses were large and strongly built of wood, thatched with the leaves of the palm-tree; they build them with two stories, the upper one being the sleeping room, and the lower the eating room.

The peculiar and unprecedented condition of these happy islanders, has always excited the most lively interest in all who have visited their hospitable village; uniting all the simplicity of the untaught savage, with the regular industry and religious feelings of cultivated society, they presented an anomaly in the human race which had never before been presented to the eye of the philosopher.

All their feelings and habits were moulded upon the patriarchal model; Adams was looked on as their chief and father, from a natural feeling of reverence for him, the oldest of the community, whose wisdom taught them how to supply those wants which they felt, and how to secure the happiness they experienced by pursuing a life of peace and concord. Being himself taught by example, his pupils profited by his experience without being exposed to the snares and temptations of corrupt society.

What would have been the result, had this society been permitted to remain unmolested on their sea-girt and rock-embattled fortress for two or three generations, it is impossible to determine; the enemy have surprised the fort, the wolf has found his way into the sheepfold!

When John Adams was dying, he called his children, as the islanders may not improperly be termed, around him, and after exhorting them to remember the good counsels he had given them, and never to fail in their religious and moral duties, he recommended them, when he was gone, to choose one from among them who should be their chief.

They did not follow this advice of the venerable patriarch, and the reason is obvious. At this time three other Englishmen, besides Adams, were residing on the island, each of whom, from his presumed superior knowledge, was by the unsophisticated simplicity of the islanders considered better fitted to command than one of themselves, and who would probably have refused to obey one of those whom they considered as their pupils. Had a choice been made among the Englishmen, there was (from their character and various pretensions) every probability of a contest for power. One of them, by marriage with Adams's daughter, was possessed of property in the island, and as such might perhaps have claimed the succession as the legitimate representative of the last chief; Buffett had long lived among them, exercising the honoured offices of their schoolmaster and spiritual teacher; whilst George Nunn Hobbs, who appears to have been an ignorant fanatic, was already disputing the latter function with Buffett.

They feared that discord and contention would result from any choice under these circumstances, and as ambition had not yet lighted her unhallowed flame on the pure altar of their innocent hearts, none among themselves attempted to claim superiority, and from the death of Adams they continued without a chief, or any authorised check upon disorder. The natural results have succeeded, and the once happy family is scattered and divided.

The island is from six to seven miles in circumference, and contains an area of about 2500 acres, one-twelfth of which only was cultivated at the time of Captain Waldegrave's visit in 1830. The population was then only 79, and Captain Waldegrave computed that the soil, if fully cultivated, would support one thousand souls, which is perhaps an excessive estimate. The soil naturally produces the cocoa-nut, plantains, bananas, yams, sweet potatoes, taro-root, the cloth-tree, the banyan (ficus Indicus), and the mulberry; the bread-fruit (brought by Christian), water-melons, pumpkins, potatoes, tobacco, the lemon, and orange, had been cultivated with success.

From remains of ancient morais, or burying-places, and some rudely carved images, and hatchets found on the island, it appears to have been formerly inhabited, but abandoned, either from the population exceeding the means of supply, or, which is quite as likely, from the death of all the inhabitants.

The dread of over-peopling their islands seems quite a disease among the inhabitants of the Polynesian islands; and to this may be attributed the institution of the detestable society of Arreoys, whose professed object is to lessen the population, which it does very effectually. Their wars are also a constant drain, and their indolent and intemperate life induces maladies which also serve to thin the population. All these causes have operated so efficiently, that there is every reason to believe that the population of the various islands was as great, if not larger, two or three hundred years ago, as it is at present; yet the dread of over-population still continues.

How different was it with the natives of Pitcairn! bred up in temperance and virtue (for the fate of Quintal and M'Koy produced its due effect), they were as remarkable for vigorous health and extraordinary muscular power, as for the rectitude of their moral conduct. It was an easy feat for the men to swim round their island; and the women, whose beauty and engaging man-

ners have been already noticed, were scarcely inferior to the men. George Young and Edward Quintal, two of the islanders, have each carried, at one time, a kedge-anchor, two sledge-hammers, and an armourer's anvil, weighing together upwards of six hundred pounds; and Quintal once carried a boat twenty-eight feet in length. They had begun to build regular keeled boats, instead of canoes, and if left to themselves would have found means of emigration when the time came, and a surplus population made such a proceeding necessary; but by their more recent visitors they appear to have been inoculated with this foolish fear of exhausting their resources, and if any are now left they are but a remnant.

In consequence of a representation made by Captain Beechey, a supply of various articles of dress and agricultural tools were sent out from Valparaiso in the Seringapatam, Capt. the Hon. W. Waldegrave, who arrived in March 1830. He found that two new visitors had come among them, John Evans, the son of a coach-maker in Long Acre, and George Nunn Hobbs; this latter had assumed the office of clergyman and schoolmaster, before exercised by Buffett, and had in fact created a sort of schism in the once peaceful society, whilst the religious doctrines he taught appeared to savour more of cant than true piety. Captain Waldegrave found that Adams had died in the preceding year, 1829. The population at the time of Captain Waldegrave's visit was estimated at 79, and already the people had begun to speculate on removing to a larger island. This idea has since been encouraged by the missionaries engaged in the South Sea Islands; and it is understood that, about three years ago, the design was carried into execution, and the inhabitants transported to Otaheite and other neighbouring islands. The destruction of such a society, so pure and so happy, cannot be contemplated without a sigh. Never perhaps was there an instance of such good seed springing from so evil a stock; and the example of Adams, who from a man of violence and blood became the venerated patriarch of a thriving colony, who owed all they knew to his care and instruction, may serve to teach a useful lesson, proving as it does that man, having the will, still has the power to retrace his steps in the path of evil, and to turn them, though tardily yet surely, to the path of good.

THE END.

CPSIA information can be obtained
at www.ICGtesting.com
Printed in the USA
BVOW03s1426210317

478937BV00030B/167/P